ACKNOWLEDGMENTS

First and foremost, we have to thank
league, and all around badass, Noah
some of our most dangerous expediti
book can be felt in every chapter.

A big thank you goes out to Joseph A. Citro for lending his expertise to this project and agreeing to write the foreword.

Another round of enormous appreciation goes out to cold weather hating Nisa Giaquinto for all of her support and advice, and all my love to Leo Lewis, the bravest kid I know.

Special thanks to Rebekah Hansen for all of her encouragement, insightful advice, and support.

Additional thanks also to Gary and Adonna Nelson for always having my back with every crazy idea I've ever had.

A big thank you to David Weatherly for adding his immense expertise to this project.

Of course, this book would not be nearly as awesome as it is without assistance from a ton of researchers, tour guides, and experts in their field including:

Britt Dahl and the rest of the amazing staff at the Roseau County Historical Museum in Roseau, Minnesota

Pearl Lorentzen and everyone at Slave Lake's *Lakeside Leader* Newspaper

The wonderful staff at the Fort Saskatchewan Museum and Historic Site

Professor Shawn Smallman who was gracious enough to answer all of our pesky emails

John Robert Colombo for providing us with some keen insight on the legend

Our colleagues Linda Godfrey and Todd Roll, who also lent their knowledge to this project

The Provincial Archives of Alberta—a treasure trove of great history

We also have to thank the numerous historical societies, research libraries, universities and public libraries that assisted us in our research. These places are truly a treasure for us all.

Wendigo Lore is a scary book to read on a cold winter's night whether or not you take your Wendigos seriously. The authors of this book do take these cannibalistic denizens of the "northern woods" seriously indeed, carefully combing the historical record for accounts of their appearances and disappearances. The text is not only illustrated, it is written with care and also in a lively manner, so it will appeal to general readers with a taste for thrills and chills as well as to students interested in Native subjects and Canadian themes.

—John Robert Colombo, author or editor of *Windigo* (1982), *Mysterious Canada* (1988), *The Mystery of the Shaking Tent* (1993), etc.

WENDIGO LORE

MONSTERS, MYTHS, AND MADNESS

WENDIGO LORE

MONSTERS, MYTHS, AND MADNESS

BY

CHAD LEWIS & KEVIN LEE NELSON

On the Road Publications

ISBN: 978-1-7338026-1-1
Printed in the United States by Documation
www.backroadslore.com

Cover Design: Kevin Lee Nelson
Back Cover Artwork by Rick Fisk
All photos taken by the authors unless noted

DEDICATION

This book is dedicated to all who lost their lives at the hands of the wendigo—whether through a monstrous attack of the body or mind.

TABLE OF CONTENTS

PREFACE

The Spelling of Wendigo

There is no one correct way to spell wendigo. Numerous variations existed based on geographic location, time period, culture, and the overall spelling prowess of those who were documenting the legend. We ultimately chose the "wendigo" spelling because it was the version that we encountered most while growing up and living in the Great Lakes area of the United States. Obviously in Canada, spelling it as "windigo" is the more common modern preference, but in the United States, the version with an "e" is most commonly used.

Others may argue that we should have used an even earlier version of the name—to which our reply is—which one? No matter what spelling we pick, there are going to be some who disagree with our choice. We also recognize that outside of the various spellings, there are completely different names given to what were/are seemingly the same creatures (Chenoo, Stone Coat, Mhuwe, etc...) encountered in different locations. Yet in order to avoid confusion, and for the sake of simplicity, we chose to use wendigo.

Here are just a few of the other various spellings of the creature: windigo, wiindigoo, weendigo, windego, wiindgoo, windgo, windago, windiga, wendego, windagoo, widjigo, wiijigoo, wijigo, weejigo, wintigo, wentigo, wehndigo, wentiko, windgoe, wintsigo. windigoag , windegoag, wiindigooag, windikouk, witiko, wihtikow.

Cultural Sensitivity

Although we cover this concern quite extensively in the Unthawing a Legend chapter, we felt its importance warranted another mention. The origin of the wendigo will forever be a First Nation legend. However, for the last several hundred years, much like humankind itself, the legend has morphed, progressed, and spread, not just in location, but in thought as well. We feel that our research, and this book, will bear out that we have treated this legend with the utmost appreciation and respect.

No Agenda

It is not our intent to try to convince or dissuade you regarding the credibility of these legends. We do not come at this legend with an agenda or purpose other than a keen appreciation for the lore. We provide commentary in places where we deem it necessary, and point out correlations or inconsistencies where we see fit, but for the most part we allow these stories and legends to exist in their natural habitat—free from over speculation or hypothesizing. In spots where the legend is complex or filled with jargon (Windigo Psychosis)—we provide an overview of the theories and trust that you will reach your own conclusion.

An Overload of Information

With nearly two decades of our own personal travel and on-site research at our disposal, combined with countless academic papers, historical newspaper articles, and a robust supply of books dealing with the subject, our greatest challenge was deciding what information would have to be cut from the book. We could have easily (and happily) made this a 1,000-page tome. However, our goal was to try to make this book a definitive guide to wendigo lore, while simultaneously keeping it easily approachable for the general public. The literature on wendigo lore is already overflowing with academic papers and books that approach the topic from an anthropological, ethnohistorical, and sociological perspective, yet nearly all fail to even remotely address the supernatural aspect of the legend. We feel our work is the first major investigation into the creature that approaches the subject as not merely fantasy or a mental illness, but an essential part of the existence of those who believed in it.

FOREWORD

By Joseph A. Citro

Can you remember your first encounter with the Wendigo?

For me it was when I was about 10 years old. The fright it gave me resulted in sleepless nights, daytime dread, and a lifelong sense of unease. Really. It was that high impact. This was 1961, the era of live TV. I had blundered into a short-lived series called *Great Ghost Tales*. At that age, of course, I knew everything about monsters and ghosts, but I had never heard a damn thing about Wendigos. "A what?" people replied when I asked around. Back then no one knew anything about Wendigos.

As I recall, the 30-minute broadcast was a totally successful exercise in tension and terror. I ignored the writer's name, but carried the disturbing scenario around with me until, as a teenager, I stumbled across the source material in a horror anthology: Algernon Blackwood's 1910 short story "The Wendigo." Reading it was an unnerving experience, though it didn't hold me in thrall the way that 30-minute B&W drama had. Something about that initial contact lodged the Wendigo firmly in my memory. Since then I have never been able to go hiking or camping without it disrupting whatever reverie I might be enjoying.

Although Mr. Blackwood's story had taken place amid the endless Canadian wilderness, and I was in Vermont, I knew I wasn't safe. The vast tracts of forest were connected and whatever walked up north knew no international boundaries. As an adult, picking up the pen to write my third horror novel—*The Gore*—Wendigo lore was very much with me. The critter became the suspect in a series of disappearances. An old man, a retired logger from Vermont's Northeast Kingdom, believed he had encountered one in the dark forests around the logging camp. When his friend vanished, the old man suspected the Wendigo had taken him. His memory of the Wendigo was nearly identical to the one I had carried around since 1961.

> *Screeching, the frost-black monster swoops down from the treetops, eyes stretched wide, bleeding from the tremendous velocity. It runs on burn-scarred limbs, deformed by its unending race through the wilderness. Jagged spikes of bone protrude from the stumpy ends of its legs where, over the years, the flesh has worn away. Its fang-filled face, only human by suggestion; splits open into a savage, lipless grin. Roaring, it grabs the black man, runs with him—screaming—into the woods. Then, with Cooly limp and powerless, it begins to feed.*

And the Wendigo was still haunting me in 2009 when I started writing *The Vermont Monster Guide*. There was little, if any, information available about Wendigos in the Green Mountain State, but I knew they were here... at least the one buried within my memory and imagination.

As I dug into my research, I realized something alarming: the Wendigo couldn't be dismissed as simply fiction. The belief was widespread among Native Americans. It had even been studied as a psychological aberration. People could transform into Wendigos, if not paranormally, then psychologically.

But with the 1961 Wendigo TV show apparently lost forever, and with my work on *The Gore* completed, and the Wendigo chapter of my *Vermont Monster Guide* done, I thought my work with this most disturbing of monsters was behind me. Sure, I wanted to learn more, but resources seemed painfully limited, and I had other projects to tackle and other things to do. Then, as if by magic, I was invited to write the Foreword for a new book.

I am delighted to be a part of the project, because *Wendigo Lore: Monsters, Myths, and Madness* contains all the material I was looking for but never found. And it will satisfy, once and forever, the myriad questions that troubled the mind of a ten-year-old boy who, long ago, had met the Wendigo for the first time.

1
THE WENDIGO: UNTHAWING A LEGEND

Wendigo. The mere mention of these monsters' names was enough to strike absolute terror, chaos, and panic into the very fabric of early First Nation life, often forcing peoples to abandon their communities until the deadly beasts had passed. For hundreds of years, wendigos have been the most frightening things ever to set foot in North America.

Fast forward to the early 2000s and the unshakable fear of the monster manifested itself in a completely new manner... the researching and writing of this book. For nearly two decades the prospect of putting out a wendigo book completely consumed and terrified Kevin and me.

By far, the wendigo would be the most complex, culturally sensitive, and puzzling legend of folklore that we had ever pursued. How would we even begin to tackle such a daunting task? On many late-night planning sessions, we frequently asked the question of whether we should even be the ones doing a book on the creature (I will discuss this dilemma in more depth below). We would begin our research and writing only to quickly expel the notion of this book from our minds. But by then, it was too late, the wendigo had already possessed us (thankfully only figuratively) and we were far too deep into the cold to simply let it go. Every year, as the brutal northern Wisconsin winters settled in, the icy voice of the wendigo would inevitably call out to us. Often a flood of travel and research would follow our new-found confidence and motivation. A few months later, when the sun began to defeat the ice, we would once

One of my first expeditions into Canada in search of the wendigo
Photo by Authors

again find ourselves putting the wendigo aside due to the debilitating realization that the legend was simply too large, too intricate, too multifaceted to ever be captured.

Yet, the more we consumed the literature, the more we traveled to speak with those who believed in, feared, and experienced the wendigo, the further we drifted from reaching any conclusions. Today, I view all those previous failed attempts at this book as a hidden blessing, knowing full well that the book we would have written 15 years ago would not be able to hold a candle to today's version. Not only have our knowledge and thoughts on the wendigo grown exponentially, so too has our overall understanding of folklore and the meaning and significance it plays in the human experience.

The only remaining stumbling block was the poignant question of whether two Caucasian men from the Midwest had the right to tackle such a profound First Nation legend. Would this be just another failed attempt at cultural appropriation? Kevin and I discussed this question ad nauseam before coming to the conclusion that we present here. Yes, unquestionably the wendigo is, and always will be, a First Nation legend, much like vampires are forever tied to Transylvania, werewolves to Europe, leprechauns to Ireland and so on and so on. Yet, all of these monsters are not simply bound by a specific culture, geographical borders, period of time, religion, gender, or belief system. They exist in the deepest recesses of the human brain; they transcend man-made labels and harken back to something darker and more sinister that dwells deep in the human mind. We believe that the absolute true nature of the beasts cannot

Twenty years into our research and we are still
digging up new information
Photo by Authors

be truly known by anyone who was not privy to First Nation winter life of 400 years ago—whether you are Native or not. That type of wendigo existed only in that space and time, adhering to those specific belief systems. There is no doubt that today's wendigo is much different than the ones inhabiting the original lore.

We also decided early on that we would forgo the usual analysis conducted by outsiders on how the wendigo was really a mental manifestation stemming from changing family roles, women's identity in a marriage, or the Canadian government's assertion of power over the First Nation people. Far too many anthropologists have trekked down this path, leading to an overflow of theories on what the wendigo is and what it is not. We, on the other hand, are approaching this book from the perspective that regardless of what modern science, sociologists, and anthropologists contend, the wendigo was absolutely real to those who lived in constant fear of it. We wanted to focus mainly on the supernatural aspects of the legend that are far too often ignored by academia.

Another factor alleviating our fears was the fact that, although the wendigo was most feared by the First Nation peoples, there were plenty of other cultures and peoples experiencing and changing the wendigo folklore as well. A wide assortment of missionaries, fur traders, and early pioneer explorers all combined their superstitions, legends, and folklore into the wendigo mix, too. After 400 plus years, the monster has become ingrained in many other cultures— including that of our own Midwestern states. The legend of the wendigo is prolific in the Great Lakes states where we were born and raised. After a lecture of mine in Minnesota a woman in her 80s talked with me. She had grown up in far northern Minnesota, and as a young girl her father used to tell her and the other village children that if they ever heard a kettle being struck in the woods, they needed to run home as fast as they could because it meant the wendigo was coming. Although she never did hear the wendigo banging its kettle, the story remained fresh in her mind some 70 plus years later. Her story demonstrates the power of the wendigo legend in our neck of the woods.

We have tried to follow in the vein of thinking from Professor Shawn Smallman, who also grappled with the question of whether another Euro-Canadian voice on the topic was needed. While writing *Dangerous Spirits: The Windigo in Myth and History*, Smallman opined that "outsiders have heard, recorded, and passed on these narratives and sought to understand these cases at least since the Jesuits arrived in New France."

It was with this thinking that the adventure began.

It was back in 2001 that I first headed up to the far northern town of Ross, Minnesota to research the odd tales told in the journal of an early pioneer named Jake Nelson. On several occasions, Nelson made a journal entry about the belief that the wendigo had visited a settlement called Indian Village. A few weeks later, I made my first expedition into the unfathomable wilds of Canada to pursue more wendigo cases and lore. In the ensuing 20 years, both Kevin and I have made countless other expeditions to the northlands of Wisconsin, Michigan, Vermont, Minnesota, and Canada in pursuit of the wendigo.

I'm glad that we were able to resist the siren-like call of the wendigo for all those early years. However, similar to those who felt they were "going wendigo," eventually the craving became too unbearable for us to handle and the wendigo project had to spring to life.

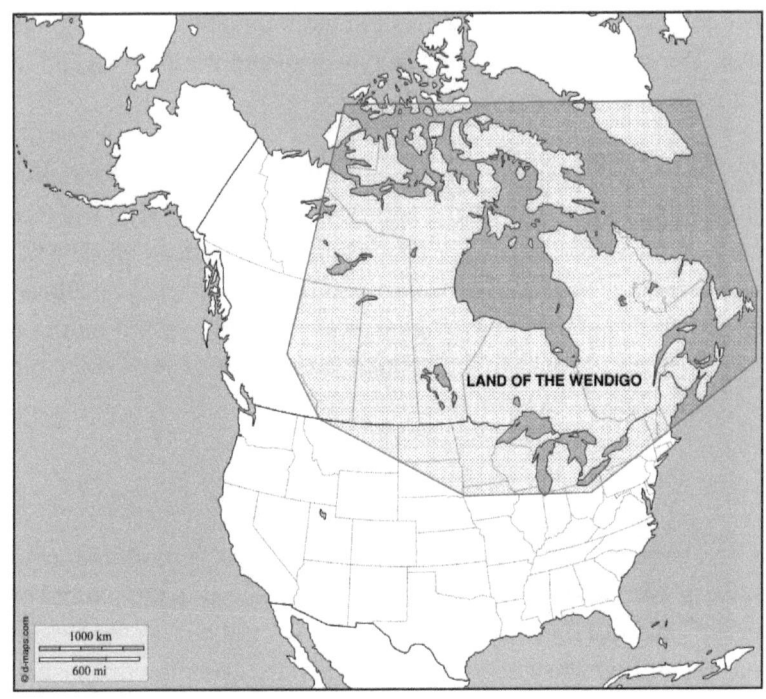

Region of wendigo traditions, beliefs, and activity

2
LAND OF THE WENDIGO

Wendigo and the Wilderness

It stalks the icy wastelands and northern boreal forests. Its howl can turn a man's blood cold. Its heart is made of solid ice—pitiless and unrelenting. It can grow to monstrous size and tower over the pines. It is mad with hunger and driven by an insatiable desire for human flesh. While there are many legends of monsters that haunt the woodlands of North America, none is more terrible than the dreaded wendigo.

Its native habitat is the boreal forests stretching from eastern Newfoundland and Labrador to the Rockies in the west, and from north of Hudson Bay down to the Great Lakes region. However, its true abode is the liminal space between myth and reality, existing with one foot in the material world and one foot in the realm of the spirits.

The vast and desolate northern wilderness is the perfect setting for a creature like the wendigo; not only perfect, but a *necessary* one. The northern landscape, with its bone-chilling cold, limited resources, and severe isolation, is a prerequisite for wendigo phenomena. Regarding the wendigo's relationship to the northern environment, anthropologist Anthony Wonderley observes, "Embodying cold and the far north, these beings were said to be reflections of their boreal forest setting." Simply put, without hostile conditions inherent to the subarctic landscape, like brutal snowstorms, frequent famine conditions, and severe melancholia induced by long winter nights in confinement, a monster like the wendigo simply could not exist. The two are intrinsically linked.

Among all cultures, and from the earliest times, the wilderness has been perceived as a place where a person was likely to get turned around, confused, or fall into a wild and deranged state—physically and mentally lost. Literally losing themselves in every way. In fact, the word "bewilder" is derived from the term "wilderness." Creative Writing professor Victoria Nelson wonderfully describes the fear of encountering raw, powerful, and elemental *otherness* in the wilderness that can lead to a sense of *mysterium tremendum*. In her article, "Seeing Wendigos," she writes, "The experience produces fear and trembling instead of joy because it puts us in the presence of something we apprehend through a faculty other than the five senses. When it invades our consciousness, we simply do not know how to contain it. The ancient Greeks and Romans, like the Algonquin and the Cree, were more familiar with this faculty than we are." Indeed, the word "panic" stems from the Greek god Pan who is the god of nature, woodlands, and mountain wilds. In his classic story, "The Wendigo" (1910) Algernon Blackwood knew all too well about the panic that the wilderness may induce and also its de-

Winter in the Northwoods
Photo by Authors

structive siren's call, writing, "For the Panic of the Wilderness had called to him in that far voice—the Power of untamed Distance—the Enticement of the Desolation that destroys."

When one is deep in the northern backcountry almost anything can seem possible. Amid the endless pines and countless lakes, the normal conventions of civilization can seem ill-equipped, irrelevant, or even laughable; while at the same time, notions and beliefs presumed impossible elsewhere may appear entirely reasonable or even *probable*. The wilderness is more than just an untamed geographical locale; it is also correlative to the hinterlands of the human psyche—the place where monsters dwell.

Environmental historian William Cronon insightfully writes, "In the wilderness the boundaries between human and nonhuman, between natural and supernatural, have always seemed less certain than elsewhere." This concept was not lost on celebrated horror writer Clive Barker when he picked the location for his mythical hamlet Midian for his horror novel *Cabal* (also adapted into the 1990 film *Nightbreed*). Midian is "where the monsters live," a wild and remote location chosen to escape mankind's notice and thereby avoid persecution. Barker teases the actual geographical location of Midian by saying, "It's northwest of Athabasca … east of Peace River, near Shere Neck, North of Dwyer." This places it in the vicinity of Slave Lake, Wabasca, and Trout Lake in Alberta, Canada —ground zero for wendigo phenomena.

In *Mysterious North* author Pierre Berton further illuminates the unique suitability the landscape has for particularly fearsome monsters writing, "The Canadian north has a fabric of mythology all its own … all indigenous to the land. The supernatural creatures who roam the tundra and the forests are all gargantuan, for the north is too immense to harbor fairy folk … the Weetigo of the Berrens, that horrible, naked cannibal, his face black with frostbite, his lips eaten away to expose his fang-like teeth." This, without a doubt, is a habitat for horrors.

In his paper "Windigo Psychosis," anthropologist Morton Teicher comments on the severe conditions of the northern wilderness and how it facilitates the wendigo process:

> The lonely and remote woodlands stretched unbrokenly, providing a rigorous and relatively resourceless physical environment in which eking out the necessities of life was a ceaseless struggle. Practically nothing could be grown and so the food quest was concentrated largely on hunting and trapping local fauna. There was a stern and merciless quality to the frozen land, making famine a constant companion. Death by starvation threatened ominously and was certainly not infrequent. In a sense, cold and hunger were the harsh geographical contributions to a cultural matrix in which food quest inevitably assumed a dominant position.

Yet, despite an inhospitable environment, indigenous Algonkians (a name referring to many distinct Native American and First Nation tribes who are linguistically linked), like the Ojibwe and Cree tribes, managed to carve out an existence in an unforgiving landscape for thousands of years. The Ojibwe and Cree are the original inhabitants of a land of "cold and hunger." They are also the people who first encountered one of the land's most terrible creatures—the wendigo. It is with them that the story of the wendigo begins.

In *The Manitous: The Spiritual World of the Ojibway* Basil Johnson explores the etymology behind the term "wendigo." Johnson states the word may be derived from *ween dagoh*, meaning, "solely for the self." Or it may originate from *weenin n'd'igoooh,* meaning "fat" or "gluttony." Considering the environmental conditions, it's easy to understand why individuals (or monsters) that only think about themselves, or who take more than they need, were seen as the epitome of evil and death. Life in subarctic communities was traditionally harsh and unforgiving (and still can be). Winter starvation was a very real and constant fear. Starvation may be far less of a concern today, but in earlier times, people had to work together and share their resources to survive. Everyone had to do their part. Cooperation, empathy, and generosity were essential to survival. Self-centered individuals who only thought of themselves were shunned or banished.

Devil in the Details
Beyond traditions and lore, oral narratives of wendigos have also left a mark on the landscape in the form of place names. Open up any map of the Great Lakes region, or almost all of Canada, and you will see scores of places containing "wendigo" in their name (or one of the dozens of spelling variants). There are thirty-two places in Ontario with Wendigo/Windigo in their name, with Wendigo Lake and Wendigo Island occurring several times. There are five in Manitoba, like Wendigo Point, Wendigo Beach, and Wendigo River. In the Great Lakes region there is Windigo Ranger Station on Isle Royale National Park, Lake Windigo in Minnesota (more on this in Chapter 7), and Windigo Lake in Wisconsin.

Indigenous people believed that spirits inhabited the land and favored certain places, usually places marked by uncommon natural features, like Lake Windigo on Star Island—a lake within a lake. Unique and unusual places were given names reflecting their spiritual status. In English, some examples translate to "Place of Spirits," "Medicine Place" (good or bad), or "Sacred Place." When European settlers arrived and encountered places named after Native spirits and indigenous magic, they interpreted them as "heathen" sites. To many Europeans, spirits of a non-Christian na-

Windigo Visitor's Center at Isle Royale National Park.
Image Courtesy of the National Park Service

ture, whether good or bad, were all devils and demons. It's easier to demonize something than take the time to learn about it. Considering the wendigo was a type of evil spirit (likely the only one from Native cosmology they were aware of), settlers named many sacred sites after the wendigo. Among early settlers the name "wendigo," or any type of "manitou," was synonymous with "devil," so besides wendigo names we also have scores of places with names like Devil's Lake, Devil's Backbone, Devil's Punchbowl, etc. Many have striking geological features (rock formations, caves, grottos, etc.), or other natural oddities, so if you're on a road-trip and see a place with Wendigo or Devil in the name, it's probably worth a side-trip.

3

WENDIGO METAMORPHOSIS: GOING WENDIGO

When we first began this project, we started with one basic question: *what exactly is a wendigo*? Answering that question proved to be far more difficult than we had originally thought. We knew early on in our research that wendigo beliefs and legends would be a tricky subject, as the vast body of case reports and oral narratives could not be pinned down and defined in simple terms. This is a common issue when dealing with monster tales originating from varied traditions, cultures, and geography. For example, let's take something like the vampire legend: Are they well-dressed, attractive, and seductive creatures of the night? Or are they hideous corpse-like revenants shambling around in their burial shroud? Are they physical flesh-and-blood beings that drink human blood? Or are they non-corporeal wraiths that steal one's life-force? It depends on whom you ask, and also, *where* and *when* you ask. Vampires are *all* of these things, and they will likely be something different a century from now. This is the nature of cultural belief systems and folklore; they can't be examined in a lab and defined in absolute terms. The same applies to the wendigo. Traditions, beliefs, and folklore are not static. They are cultural systems that are continually redefined and colored by the backgrounds and beliefs of those who are closely engaged with them.

While researching nearly three centuries of wendigo lore we found descriptions of wendigos generally fell into three distinct categories: a malevolent spirit-like entity, a mad human driven to cannibalism, or a large non-human (or no longer human) ogre-like monster. Naturally, this led to some confusion about what a wendigo even is, as all are considered a wendigo. So, are there three distinctly different types of wendigo? The answer is not that simple. Separating them shows a failure to understand how all three are intrinsically linked. For example, a caterpillar is distinct from a butterfly, yet they are in essence the same organism. They are two different, and very distinct, stages of its life cycle. A similar process applies to the wendigo, as one needs to look at the varied types as stages of a linear process (an unfortunate development for the afflicted individual). A wendigo can be any of these three stages; it just depends upon where it currently exists in its development. Algonkian traditions indicate that some (if not most) giant wendigos were once humans who were spiritually attacked, possessed, and driven to madness and cannibalism. Once they had eaten human flesh, they began a metamorphosis into a literal monster. Thus, the wendigo in its most monstrous form could be considered a *late-stage* wendigo. It's a complex but fascinating system of beliefs that we will explore in more detail in this chapter.

Dreaming of Wendigo

Powerful and transformative dreams play a fundamental role in wendigo lore, and ultimately, in the creation of new wendigos. They are the earliest indicator of impending wendigo syndrome, an early-warning sign that an individual is under spiritual attack. Among Cree, Métis, Ojibwe, and other Algonkian tribes, dreams are seen as just as important, if not *more* important, than the waking world. They have the power to transform individuals by giving them powers and insight. Generally, transformative powers conferred via dreams are a positive boon, such as an uncanny understanding of wild game roaming patterns, instinctive knowledge of medicinal plants, or a newly-awakened fearlessness in battle. In rarer cases, dream transformations can be detrimental. They can be the first sign marking the initial stage of the wendigo process.

First, let's discuss how sacred dreams are received, why they are sought, and under what conditions. The process begins at puberty with males. When a boy reaches puberty, he is instructed to fast and spend time alone outside the village. His goal is to seek a sacred vision that will come in the form of a dream. This is done in the spring when the snow is melting. It is a rite of passage where a young man is forced to leave childhood behind, face his fears, and figure out what sort of man he will be. Each person's experience is different. While in a trance state, induced by hunger and fears of being alone in the wilderness, young men wait to make contact and receive a message from their personal *pawagan* (dream visitor), or *manitou*— spirit guardians and tutelary beings who come in dreams to bring blessings and powers. They are regarded as one's patron spirit. It is believed that a person's life will not be successful or reach its full potential without the assistance of their spiritual helper. Each person is linked to a specific pawagan at birth, but they usually remain hidden, making themselves initially known only during the vision quest. Some individuals who have a particularly strong connection to their pawagan may experience dream encounters with them prior to their fasting ceremony, or they may already feel a strong connection to a particular tutelary spirit, or affinity with a particular spirit animal, so when the spirit reveals itself it is not always a surprise.

There are many types of pawaganak (plural), and they fall into three general categories. All are individual entities with proper names rather than classifications, or types, of entities. First, some pawaganak are anthropomorphic beings from Native mythology, often mythic heroes and trickster characters like Wisakedjak and Wenabozho. The second class are the masters of animal species. There are pawaganak for every type of animal, bird, and fish in the forest, and each has its own traits, personality, and powers. They are the "boss" animal spirit—the original and eternal counterpart of a particular type of animal. They are the type of spirit most commonly encountered in the fasting ritual and are representative of common animals: Rabbit, Turtle, Wolf, etc, (proper names). The nature of the pawagan's form (the animal class it rules) is indicative of what one's station in society will be. Young men who have Bear or Wolf for their pawagan are likely destined to be good hunters and warriors, while Turtle often appears to future healers. They are usually useful, but not always. If one dreams of Porcupine one must be extra careful because of its relationship to the wendigo. If they are offered porcupine meat in the dream, they must refuse it, for it is a test. If the dreamer consumes the meat, he will become a wendigo and lose his blessing from the Porcupine pawagan.

Another linkage between porcupines and wendigos is the belief that the porcupine is one of the wendigo's creatures. Therefore, one must never kill a porcupine idly or risk angering a wendigo. Among the Cree and Ojibwe, the porcupine is especially revered. It is a bold animal that trundles noisily through the forest because it has no fear of other animals. With its formidable quills a porcupine can even fend off a hungry wolf. Decorative porcupine quills are sewn into moccasins to imbue them with the strength of the animal. Even in the waking world it is believed that if you eat porcupine you risk turning into a wendigo. One cautionary tale tells of how some men threw a porcupine heart into a cooking pot after they had already eaten. Another hunter arrived, and, being very hungry, ate the remaining food in the pot. Later that night in the tent the porcupine-eater turned into a wendigo and ate one of the other men (the one who threw in the heart).

Sometimes pawaganak are dangerous, either by their unpredictable and volatile nature, or because they are well-known villains, or beings of the underworld, in Native cosmology. The third class of pawaganak are semi-human entities representing spirits of creatures that are mythic in nature, like Paguak, (a flying skeleton spirit), Thunderbird (a mythic ruler of the upper world), Memegwesi (dwarf-like creatures believed to inhabit caves along riverbanks), various underworld spirits like the Water Panther, and even Wendigo.

It should be noted that the concept of the Wendigo spirit can be confusing, especially for those not familiar with Native belief systems and cosmologies. Within the spiritual realm, there is a primary (or eternal) Wendigo spirit. This is often viewed as a single mythic entity where Wendigo (capital "W") is a proper name. It is similar to the difference between the Devil (proper name) and 'devils'—they are separate entities but also spiritually linked. Often wendigo spirits are discussed in a plural sense, as there can be many, but they all are parts of the primary Wendigo. This is a feature of the spiritual realm; it doesn't have the same hard and fast rules as the physical world. Thus, Wendigo can simultaneously be a single primary being, or it can be a multitude of wendigo spirits. The primary Wendigo pawagan entity can make wendigos for sorcerers to send against their enemies. They are essentially minor parts of itself that possess a victim and turn them into cannibal monsters. Being less powerful than the primary Wendigo, they can be conjured against, battled, and defeated by other sorcerers and their pawagan spirit allies. In contrast, the primary Wendigo is eternal and can be defeated only by other ancient and original spirits.

Contact with dangerous pawaganak is seen as potentially rewarding, but also perilous to the individual, for, as they say, *with power comes responsibility*. Whereas Thunderbird (commanding the power of storms and lightning) may appear to a future Chief, Wendigo may appear to a future sorcerer. One documented wendigo account attributed the person's wendigo transformation to their pawagan. In this case, Frost was their pawagan (Frost is sometimes used interchangeably with Wendigo due to their mutual connection with cold/ice). Pawaganak cannot be chosen; they choose you. If one ends up with a negative or dangerous pawaganak they cannot be rejected or banished unless it chooses to abandon the individual. Instead, they must be carefully managed and regulated over a life-time.

Once one's pawagan has been revealed, young men go back to their village and announce their results. Men must be completely honest about their experience. Sometimes fasting rituals fail and one's pa-wagan does not appear. When this occurs, they must be truthful about the experience. This is not a source of shame, as the spirits are believed to have their own mysterious plan. The individual may simply have not been ready. Lying about one's pawagan is believed to cause certain disaster and is an insult to one's pawagan. It is also a sign of great disrespect to the community. The Ojibwe and Cree believe that secrets are toxic. If the results are withheld the secret will manifest in misfortune, usually as sickness in one's family, or continual bad luck in hunting and fishing. Either can be cataclysmic in tribes that rely closely on wild game for their survival.

Women can obtain guardian spirits too, but not through the sacred fast. Their discovery of their pawagan, if at all, is often a random encounter. Typically, they are not sought out by women; instead, discoveries are usually accidental, but not on the part of the pawa-gan. They reveal themselves for a reason. Women are not required to reveal their personal pawagan, and this gives them a measure of power. One never knows if they may secretly have an immensely powerful pawagan at their disposal. In *Ojibwe Stories from the Upper Berens River*, Ojibwe informant Adam Bigmouth describes an incident where a small group of women killed two wendigos. When returning from a hunting trip two men saw giant footprints in the snow heading towards their camp where they had left their wives and children. Concerned the women and children could be in danger, they quickened their pace hoping to catch the wendigo before it threatened their families. When they arrived, they saw the camp was in disarray as if a battle had taken place. Tents were torn and birch bark canoes were smashed. They thought they were too late until they saw their wives sitting by a tent calmly rocking their cradleboards (baby-carriers). Not far from the tent two giant wendigos lay dead. Then they knew the women had extremely powerful pawaganak. It was their pawaganak that had destroyed the wendigos. No one knew what the women were capable of before this happened. Adam Bigmouth adds, "Of course a lot of times it was found out that a woman was *much* stronger through dreams than a man. The reason they were so strong was because no one knew what they had dreamed—*everything was secret until the time came when they needed their helper.*"

Even if one is not chosen by the Wendigo pawagan, minor wendigo spirits may still come to people in dreams. According to traditional Native beliefs, if one dreams of a wendigo one is in danger of becoming one themselves. Dreams often include imagery of ice, blizzards, and cold. It is not uncommon for people to dream of the spirits that govern the cardinal directions, but to dream of Kiwetin (spirit of the North) is considered as an ominous sign and could be an omen for turning wendigo. Wendigo dreams are an early warning sign for susceptible individuals, or those already along the path, of becoming wendigos. At this stage some sing or make sacrifices to appease the spirit and ward it off. Sometimes it is successful, other times not.

In dreams the dreamer is frequently offered food by the wendigo spirit, often appearing as normal game food, like beaver or moose, but it's a trick. It is actually human flesh disguised as common meat. If dreamers allow themselves to be tricked into consuming the flesh they will be possessed by the wendigo and eventually turn into one. The "Trojan feast" concept is a common feature in folklore and mythologies worldwide. In many ways it is similar to European fairy lore where it is thought that if someone trespasses into a glen held sacred to fairies, the interloper will be tempted with food and drink.

If one gives into temptation, they will be trapped forever in the fairy realm. In wendigo dreams the dream-food serves as a catalyst for wendigo possession and eventual metamorphosis. It is a spiritual corruption that opens the door to possession.

The Wendigo spirit is hunger and cold personified. In the Native world, together these often meant death, which is why Wendigo is often associated with both physical death and the death of one's humanity. It is their personified nature that makes pawaganak spirits, like Wendigo, somewhat analogous to the Western concept of demons—not the one-dimensional bogeymen used in modern Christianity; rather, they are akin to the original Greek *daimons* who were personified spirits of abstract concepts, or spirits linked to a specific place. Examples include Hygeia (personification of health), Lyssa (personification of rage), and Phobos (personification of fear). Perhaps the Greek daimons aligning closest to Wendigo are Adephagia (gluttony), Limos (hunger), and Thanatos (death). Like pawaganak, daimons can be either helpful or dangerous based upon their nature and have the ability to take possession of people. Possession may manifest positively as helpful guidance from beneficent spirits, or disastrously through the total loss of Self. It is through such possession that a wendigo—the personification of cold and hunger—attempts to bind itself to a human host. If successful, the unfortunate victim is lost.

Wendigo Possession
After dreams of ice and cold, the next stage of wendigo metamorphosis is possession by a wendigo entity. The Cree of northwestern Manitoba use the verb *pihciskow* to describe possession of this variety. Wendigo spirits usually attack victims when they are in a spiritually weakened state, typically initiated by winter starvation conditions, a debilitating spiritual wound caused by a self-inflicted cultural transgression, or through a magical attack that compromises one's spiritual protection. Of the three, starvation is one of the most

common features in wendigo possession, but it is not an essential component. There are many cases of individuals going wendigo with plenty of food available. In such cases, victims do not recognize normal food as edible, or find it repulsive. Instead, they have a growing fixation and hunger for human flesh. It should be noted that they do not necessarily have a desire to kill and eat *people* per se. Instead, while in a delusional state, family and friends no longer appear as humans. To the possessed, people frequently appear as normal game animals, so to their fevered mind they are killing wild game, not committing murder. There are many accounts of the possessed stating that friends and family members look like "tasty beavers." Statements like this are somewhat reminiscent of the old cartoons depicting starving castaways in a lifeboat. One castaway looks at the other and sees a talking hot dog or other foods. While the idea may seem comical, in many wendigo cases the results were often quite the opposite and ended in brutal murders.

Once possessed, states of lucidity come and go, and the victim will fall into a depressive melancholic state. Frequently they become withdrawn, stop eating, and stop speaking. They may go through periods of high anxiety and manic episodes followed by near catatonic states. In modern terms, one could describe it as a very extreme mixture of seasonal affective disorder (SAD) and cabin fever. While in a manic state they may become violent and difficult to control. Victims may flail about and rave about terrible visions, revealing their paranoia and fears of spiritual and bodily invasion. They feel cannibalistic urges welling up inside them and feel powerless to control their own actions. In many cases victims beg to be tied up, or even killed, fearing they pose grave danger to friends and family members. One can only imagine the stress, anxiety, and terror experienced by loved ones. Within the cultural paradigm the clock is ticking. They know that if possession is allowed to take root it will put the family, and even the entire community, in danger—a truly terrible and unimaginable responsibility. If allowed to progress, even women and children could pose a real danger, becoming so powerful that they can no longer be controlled and restrained by even the strongest men and powerful shamans.

Interestingly, old women were the most feared group when it came to turning wendigo. In tribal cultures age is associated with increased power, and the secret power of women (like their unknown pawagan) makes them unpredictable and not to be underestimated. Thus, with an older female wendigo one couldn't accurately assess the level of danger until it was too late. In one case near Poplar River, Canada, a minister asked that a stricken elderly woman be delivered to a local asylum. The local chief, William Berens, stated he would require fifteen men to get her there and to ensure *their* safety, not *hers*. They weren't taking any chances. On March 16, 1888, the *Fort Wayne Sentinel*, ran an article with the headline, "CANNIBAL: Twelve Persons Said to Have Been Killed and Eaten by a Woman." The article reads,

> WINNIPEG, March 16. - A case of cannibalism reported from the Peace river country last summer turns out not to be caused by hunger, but the work of a woman who became 'wehtigo' several years ago, and has since killed and eaten twelve persons, members of her own family and others. She was alive at last accounts from Edmonton. The Indians and half breeds express surprise that the government does not arrest and punish her for her crime.

Another symptom of possession is swelling of the body. Indigenous reports often describe victims as "growing large." As the wendigo power moves through them they feel as if they are growing larger and becoming stronger. One of the most graphic accounts of this sort of physical change comes from the diary of Hudson's Bay Company clerk, Francis Work Beatton, in 1897. Beatton was at the

Trout Lake incident where a Cree man named Napanin underwent a horrific wendigo metamorphosis. Beatton's diary states, "He says his heart is freezing. He is always saying that he is going to be a cannibal. . . . He wants them to kill him all the time before he gets worse. . . . He seemed to be getting worse all the time. He does not

Artwork by RF Pangborn

look like a human being. He seems to be terribly swollen in the body and face. I do not know how this will end. The sight of him is enough to frighten any person. . . . The sound of him was terrible. He was calling like a wild bull." They tried to keep Napanin tied down for his protection (and theirs) over the course of several weeks, but he kept breaking his bonds. Once they were out of rope and any means to restrain him, they had no choice other than to kill him. His execution was justified by the fear that if he got loose, he would kill them all (see Chapter 4 for more on the Trout Lake incident).

There are many documented cases of victims describing their perilous condition, and they are remarkably compelling in their consistency. In most cases victims describe a sensation of feeling like their heart is being slowly frozen or turning to ice. This is not a metaphorical statement, nor is it a poetic way of saying one is becoming a "cold-hearted killer"; they believe their heart is literally being frozen or encased in ice. People have reported hearing mysterious sounds coming from within victims' chests that sound like ice popping under pressure, or the sound of ice crunching and scraping. In some cases, victims state their backbone is turning to ice. Stranger still is how witnesses, or wendigo hunters, have backed up these statements (after the death of the victim). Numerous accounts state that after a wendigo was killed their heart (or spine) was found to be encased in ice. Hearts are traditionally removed and burned (to melt the ice), along with the rest of the body, to ensure they do not rise from the dead. We have endeavored to find if perhaps "ice" has a dual or symbolic meaning in Ojibwe/Cree culture for a known medical condition, but we have found none. Cases of victims vomiting ice, or ice found in the chest cavity post-mortem, has us utterly perplexed. At this point, we can only take witnesses at their word.

During the possession stage it is critical victims are cured before they can act upon their urge to consume human flesh. Once they've engaged in cannibalism the wendigo metamorphosis is irreversible. Prior to that, the most common remedy is forcing victims to drink hot tallow (usually bear grease, a prudent energy-packed remedy for starvation and malnourishment). It is believed hot animal fat will help melt the ice forming around the victim's heart and hopefully help them regain their appetite for conventional food. If nothing else, it may pull them from the brink of starvation. If available, spiritual leaders, like a local shaman, are brought in to conjure out the spirit.

In some turn-of-the-century cases the services of priests were called upon to perform a similar role. Individuals were usually brought to a mission where a priest would pray for their souls. Others were delivered to asylums for psychiatric treatment. Both approaches were generally successful when administered early enough. The simple act of removing someone from a lonely and bleak environment (imagine being snowbound in a cabin or wigwam out in the wilderness) is bound to have some restorative effects. Access to nutritious food and plenty of rest are likely contributing factors in their recovery, too. (For more on wendigo curing techniques see Chapter 10).

Before I continue, it is worth noting how Ojibwe/Cree cultures function with the seasons, particularly in winter, as it may shed some light on the perilous conditions they faced and how isolation could prey upon the mind. In warmer seasons members of tribes come together and build wigwams at a communal gathering site. It is during this time that food is relatively accessible and abundant, like fish, berries, and other seasonable edibles. There is enough food in the area to sustain the whole tribe at a single location. However, as the weather gets colder, as plants wither, water sources freeze over, and as preserved food supplies dwindle, they have to rely more and more on fresh meat to survive. Naturally, there is a finite amount of game within the range of a centralized village. Most larger animals, like moose, are scared off by large scale human activity. So, in the fall the tribe fragments into smaller self-reliant units consisting of about 12-15 individuals. They spread out and live in relative isolation until the spring. By spreading out they are able to hunt a much wider area out of necessity. Most groups interact little, if at all, with other groups during the winter due to distance and harsh weather conditions, therefore they are functionally alone and have to rely upon themselves for all their needs and emergencies that may arise.

It's easy to understand how isolating conditions, during the darkest time of the year, and combined with heightened food anxiety, could prey upon one's mind. It's an optimal setting for wendigo possession to set in, particularly if hunting has not been successful. In *Ojibwa Religion and the Midewiwin,* cultural anthropologist Ruth Landes captures the brutal environmental realities and the struggles indigenous people faced with otherworldly forces when she states, "The elemental conflict of man against a hostile nature has nowhere been enacted more dramatically than in the experience of the Ojibway Indians of southwestern Ontario and northern Minnesota, where the hunter, isolated by his vast lands and frozen winters, felt himself a soul at bay, against cosmic forces personalized as cynical or terrorizing."

Wendigo Sorcery
Outside of famine conditions, people can also set themselves up for wendigo possession through self-inflicted spiritual sickness triggered by selfish behavior or careless actions. Among the Ojibwe and Cree, breaking cultural taboos can wound a person's spirit, or even negatively affect family members and future generations. It is like bringing a curse upon yourself and your family through irresponsible or excessively prideful behavior. Additionally, keeping important secrets from others is viewed as a serious transgression. In a culture where everyone relies heavily upon others for their survival this makes perfect sense. Secrets and grudges can tear at the

Wendigo Amulet
Image Courtesy of the American Museum of
Natural History, New York City

fabric of society. Holding dark secrets, anger, and resentment inside
is like having poison inside one's body. It slowly makes a person
sick, and sick people cannot perform needed duties for their community. Spirit and body are fundamentally linked. If someone has
a spiritual sickness it will also manifest in their body through pain
or other symptoms of illness. If one is spiritually sick, they are vul-
nerable for wendigo possession.

Misuse of sacred rituals or performing forbidden acts is also potentially spiritually wounding. For example, if a person who is not

trained in proper shamanic techniques tries to communicate with spirits, they risk damaging themselves spiritually. It is like playing with fire. Even those who have many years of training in spirit work, and take respectful precautions, may still open themselves up to the possibility of something going wrong, especially if they are too reckless out of hubris. For an untrained novice, attempting to conjure and perform spirit work is to invite disaster. They open themselves up to wendigo possession or harm from other powerful pawaganak.

Another example is unsanctioned divination. A popular divination technique among shamans is scapulimancy, that is, the art of divining the future through charred scapulae or speal bones. Typically, this is performed using a deer or elk shoulder blade that has been scorched by fire. The shaman then reads the array of cracks and formations in the bone like a road map. The technique is often used to determine the migration patterns of animals. Through the charred patterns the shaman is able to decipher where game will be found and increase the odds of a successful hunt. It is a sacred gift and not to be abused. The untrained, and especially children, are explicitly forbidden from attempting to read the bones. It is an insult to the spirit of the animal that provided the bone. To do so is to bring misfortune and attract the attention of harmful pawaganak, especially the wendigo.

Sorcery plays an important and prominent role in many Algonkian societies. Not surprisingly, a shaman's power is often assessed by their success rate. Power is also determined by how many pawaganak of different types a shaman can summon to assist him in his goals. This is usually performed through the shaking tent ceremony. In preparation for the ceremony a shaman will order the construction of a small conical tent made with a framework of specific trees and covered in animal hides. Usually the footprint of the tent is only big enough for the shaman, who is usually seated. The tent posts are embedded deep into the ground and held together by wood hoops. Typically, the number of posts is 6-8, but powerful shamans will sometimes build tents with over a dozen posts. This is important, because the more posts the tent contains the more difficult it is to shake. Therefore, if an extremely sturdy tent is able to shake and bend (sometimes the top will bend almost to the ground) it is proof that spirits are present. Once the shaman enters the sacred space of the tent it will usually begin to shake immediately, sometimes wildly. Incantations are sung to request an audience of spirits.

The pawaganak are said to gather and sit on the hoops near the top of the tent. They are often described as looking like "little people" or "points of light." As the spirits arrive, they announce their presence by speaking in different voices and will answer the questions of the shaman and those gathered outside the tent. Each Pawagan has a distinct personality. For example, Turtle is often very comical and speaks with a gurgling voice as if he is underwater. Early Canadian fur trader and explorer, Alexander Henry "The Younger" (1765-1814), witnessed a shaking tent ceremony. He commented that it seemed as though multiple voices were coming from the tent, "Some yelling, some barking like dogs, some howling like wolves and in this horrible concert were mingled screams and sobs, as of despair, anguish and the sharpest pain. Articulate speech was also uttered, as if from human lips, but in a tongue unknown to any in the audience."

It's common for spectators to test shamans by asking questions they couldn't possibly know, like the location of lost articles, or the well-being of distant relatives. When difficult questions are answered correctly, or miraculous feats are performed, it is believed the pawaganak are truly present. In one instance a shaman demonstrated his power by producing fresh blueberries in the dead of winter—a gift from the spirits.

Sometimes victims of wendigo possession are not the result of situational circumstances, like famine or irresponsible behavior. Sometimes they are intentionally targeted through sorcery. The entry point is still via spiritual weakness, but in the cases of wendigo sorcery the weakness is the result of a spiritual assault from a sorcerer. A powerful shaman is very respected but also feared and viewed with a measure of suspicion. They are not to be trifled with. If a person with a degree of spiritual power feels slighted or disrespected, they may choose to target their perceived enemy with a magical attack as retribution. There are many cases in which people have been targeted for wendigo possession by the actions of a sorcerer. In cases of wendigo sorcery, it is believed that wendigos are entities made out of a sorcerer's dream. They are controlled by the sorcerer and sent out to do its bidding.

In our research we discovered one of the most common reasons for magical attack was when a shaman felt insulted after being denied a request for a wife. In Algonkian societies it is common for men to have multiple wives. A few of these cases are described by Adam Bigmouth in *Ojibwe Stories from the Upper Berens River*. In one case a powerful conjurer asked to marry a young woman but was denied by her father because he felt the conjurer already had enough wives, and also because she was promised to another. The insulted suitor decided to get even. The sorcerer made an effigy of the woman out of snow, dipped it in water, and put it out in the cold to freeze solid. Next, he buried the effigy in ashes and called upon the wendigo spirit to inhabit the woman using the effigy as a mystical link. He told the father that she would not live long with her future husband and she would destroy him. He was right. The woman was soon married, but shortly after the marriage ceremony she began to fall ill. She wouldn't eat and eventually became feverish and complained of having dreams of ice. This went on for weeks. Finally, one day when her husband came home from hunting, she sprang upon him and killed him with an axe. By the time others arrived on the scene she had already eaten half of the man's back. It was clear she had gone wendigo. They had no other choice than to kill her with an axe and burn her body (more on the proper way to kill wendigos in Chapter 11). Like the effigy in the possession of the sorcerer, the poor woman's remains now rested among the ashes.

In another case a father denied a suitor because he felt his daughter was not old enough. Some weeks later the daughter returned home during the afternoon to find her mother still in bed with her infant sibling. She thought it was odd that she would still be in bed at such a late hour, so she called for her to get up. The mother would not move, yet the daughter could see the child moving under the blanket. When she went to rouse her, she found her mother's body cold and lifeless. She threw off the blanket and found the infant covered in blood. It had gone wendigo and was eating the mother. The wendigo child had already eaten one breast and was working on the other. She ran to another camp that was close by to seek help. They came back to the home and killed the wendigo. After it was dead, they noticed ice had formed along the child's backbone. It was believed the wendigo spirit had been sent as revenge by the insulted suitor.

Some magical assaults are direct, like the ones described above. In other cases, they are indirect, making it difficult to place blame upon the offended conjurer. Instead of summoning a wendigo spirit and sending it directly at a victim, conjurers will instead instruct the wendigo spirit to scare away all the game from the area surrounding a camp. It's a slower process, but the end results are the same. After a long series of unsuccessful hunts, the cursed camp will slowly begin to starve. Then, one-by-one, people become weak and open themselves up to wendigo possession. If one of them is possessed, and not cured in time, the entire camp could perish.

Explorer George Nelson (1786–1859) encountered many similar stories during the time he spent among the Ojibwe. Nelson believed in the supernatural and the Cree and Ojibwe ability to communicate with spirits. In regards to wendigo sorcery he commented, "There is such a singular, strange, and incomprehensible contradictoriness in almost all of these cases, and many I have heard, that I do most verily believe they are denunciations, witch or wizardisms: in any other manner they are not to be rationally accounted for."

There are also cases of rival sorcerers using wendigos and other spirits to battle each other. In *The Role Of Conjuring in the Salteaux Society,* A. Irving Hallowell describes one such case:

> A conjurer may likewise summon to his lodge the soul of a rival conjurer or one he believes to have done him injury, for a showdown. Each conjurer then summons all his pawaganak in turn and there is a battle royal between the opposing sides. It is a dramatic struggle to the death, right before the eyes of the audience.

> I was told a story about a contest between conjurers in which my interpreter's great-grandfather, Yellow Legs, *Uzauwaskoat,* was victorious. There was a conjurer by the name of Lynx Head, *Pijiustigwan,* who lived on the Winnipeg River, 150 miles to the south. He was very powerful, but he was a bad one, too. During the winter he starved out Yellow Legs by sorcery and one of the latter's children died.

It's an amazing story. Yellow Legs called upon another conjurer, his cousin *Ndabazis,* to help him destroy Lynx Head. He agreed, and they ordered two conjuring tents to be built. Each tent was made with forty poles, an astounding number and symbolic of their great power. During the battle each of their tents "shook like trees in a storm." Eventually, after a long battle, Lynx Head began to lose strength. Everyone could tell because his tent began to shake less and less. They heard him moaning and crying as the end drew near. Finally, the tent became still. Lynx Head was found dead inside the next morning.

Conjurers are also sought out for their ability to protect people from dangers of a supernatural order, including wendigos. According to Hallowell, "A powerful conjurer is able to protect a whole community or specific individuals from malevolent influences. He can determine the source of magically projected illness and even retaliate in kind if he is strong enough. Or he may protect a whole community from the ravages of a windigo." If a wendigo is reported approaching a community (sometimes seen in a dream), a conjurer, with the help of his pawaganak, may attempt to stop the wendigo through magical combat. Conjurers have been known to ward them off by magically hiding their camp, or by tricking the wendigo, so that it changes course and avoids the encampment. If an encounter is unavoidable, they may engage in a magical battle. A conjurer may be able to kill a wendigo if his pawaganak are more powerful than the wendigo (or the rival conjurer who sent it). Once the wendigo is defeated, the pawaganak will spiritually devour and absorb the wendigo. However, if the conjurer is not strong enough, the community is doomed. According to indigenous narratives, if not stopped, a single wendigo can wipe out an entire tribe. This is said to have happened at a place near Sandy Lake, Ontario, called Ghost Point. It was once the site of a thriving village until it was destroyed by a wendigo.

One of Hallowell's informants recounts a battle between a conjurer and a wendigo. He recalls, "During a terrific blizzard a windigo was reputed to be advancing from the north. The Indians were so terrified that they moved their wigwams to the south side of the river for several days. During all this time their strongest conjurer was at work day and night overcoming the giant cannibal which was threatening them." A similar report is examined in "Northern Algonkian Cannibalism and Windigo Psychosis" by Charles A. Bishop where he points to records in the Hudson's Bay Company archives written by Charles McKenzie of the Lac Seul post in 1837. Bishop cites McKenzie's report documenting the arrival of, "Over one hundred Indians who were fleeing in terror from a Windigo which several had reported seeing at their lakeside summer camp. They camped next to the store, posted guards, and for a week the medicine men engaged in conjuring to ward off the evil monster." It's worth noting that McKenzie also recorded descriptions of the creature from some of the Indian hunters. They described it as covered with hair and lacking heels, the latter perhaps indicating they walked on their forefeet like animals.

Artwork by Eric Franer

Cannibal Giants with Hearts of Ice

Once people who are possessed by a wendigo spirit have tasted human flesh, they begin an irreversible physical metamorphosis into wendigo monsters. This is the final stage of a ghastly process. Wendigo monsters are described in a variety of ways with slight differences between regions, but there are a number of traits that are consistent. Typically, wendigos in their monstrous form are tall, sometimes *very* tall. The more they eat, the bigger and more dangerous they get. Therefore, the older the wendigo, the larger and more frightful it will be. Older wendigos are described as standing taller than the treetops. They move like icy juggernauts through the forest. There are many tales of wendigos uprooting trees and throwing aside boulders in their path as they rampage through the wilderness. At this point their heart is frozen and entirely encased in ice. It is because of this feature that wendigos are sometimes called "ice hearts." In *Where the Chill Came From—Cree Windigo Tales and Journeys*, Howard Norman states, "Some Swampy Cree elders maintain that the giant with its heart of ice and the Windigo's human form can be the same person; that is, the two forms represent metamorphic counterparts. Both forms of wendigo are killed the same way: melting the heart."

Wendigos are invariably deathly thin and lanky. Most descriptions say their skin is pulled tightly over their bones in a continual state of starvation. It's interesting that their skinniness never equates to being weak or fragile; just the opposite, and this is what makes them so supernaturally creepy. They are thin and emaciated, yet they are still unnaturally powerful and dangerous. Like vampires, their gaunt forms belie how strong and deadly they really are. In some folkloric tales, they are described as so thin they can only be seen head-on because if viewed from the side they would be almost invisibly thin. Their skin is often jaundiced, gray, or even blackened with frostbite, and hardened like ice, making them near-invulnerable to conventional weapons. Some are said to even sweat blood. Tales mention how wendigos often chew away their own lips out of hunger. Add to that gruesome grin a mouth full of crooked yellow teeth with long fangs and you have a truly chilling visage.

Tales vary on how much hair wendigos have. This could be due to the age or sex of the wendigo, but often they are described as mostly bald, or with stringy/patchy hair (typical signs of malnourishment and starvation). Some stories describe wendigos having pale fur covering their bodies, while others mention they have hair sprouting out of their back that looks like "rabbit fur."

They behave like wild animals and are impervious to the elements; therefore, they have no need for clothes. Their nakedness is an indicator of their feral state—beasts of the forest. A wendigo's supernatural fortitude gives them immunity to cold, the bites of insects, and the lacerations of thorns and brambles. Another indicator of their wild and lowly existence is their general filthiness, as they are often covered in tree sap, pine needles, moss, and other woodland debris. In the eastern side of the continent it is said they cover themselves in pine pitch and roll in sand. Layers of sap and sand give their skin a hard and stony appearance. This is why some cannibal giants, particularly among the Iroquois, are called "Stone Coats."

Powers of the Wendigo
Throughout wendigo lore there are a few themes that are consistent between tribes and regions. Foremost of these is the creature's close association with specific elements—namely, cold and ice, which play a large role in shaping its supernatural powers. Wendigos are the personification of winter and all the grim hardships the season brings. Other powers, abilities, and associations vary from region to region.

The Fiend of Winter:
The wendigo is closely linked to the winter season, a bleak and often brutal time of the year where in earlier times the struggle

against starvation was a constant concern. Winter is the time of year when wendigos are the most active, as they are a manifestation of cold temperatures and wintry conditions. Wendigos are believed to be able to control the weather and bring howling winds and blizzards with them as they rampage through the wilderness. Because wendigos are usually portrayed as mindless marauders, some stories indicate that storms and whiteout conditions are more like an innate area effect rather than a controlled and intentional power. The wendigo is closely associated with Kawatin, the spirit of the North Wind, and is sometimes described as traveling, or flying, on the arctic winds from the North.

There are stories of wendigos attacking in the summer months, but they are exceedingly rare. According to legend, wendigos follow the snow and ice. They move south from the colder arctic regions during the five moons of winter, extending as far south as the season's snow belt. Then, as spring approaches and the days become warmer and longer, they retreat back with the melting snow. Among many tribes it is taboo to even mention the wendigo during the summer months, as it falls under the *aadizookaanan* type of story, a story that is told only in the winter to preserve its transformative power.

Dominion Over Water and Ice:
Wendigos have a supernatural connection to ice and frost. The Wendigo spirit is sometimes used synonymously with the Frost pawagan, or manitou. A wendigo's skin is frozen like ice, making it hard and tough, and impervious to arrows or bullets. Frost has worked its way through its body, encasing its heart in ice. It is the personification of icy and inhospitable conditions.

Among many tribes, children are told not to eat snow or ice out of fear that a wendigo spirit may use the ice to gain a foothold inside them. Even today in parts of northern Minnesota children are discouraged from making snowmen out of fear that a wendigo may in-

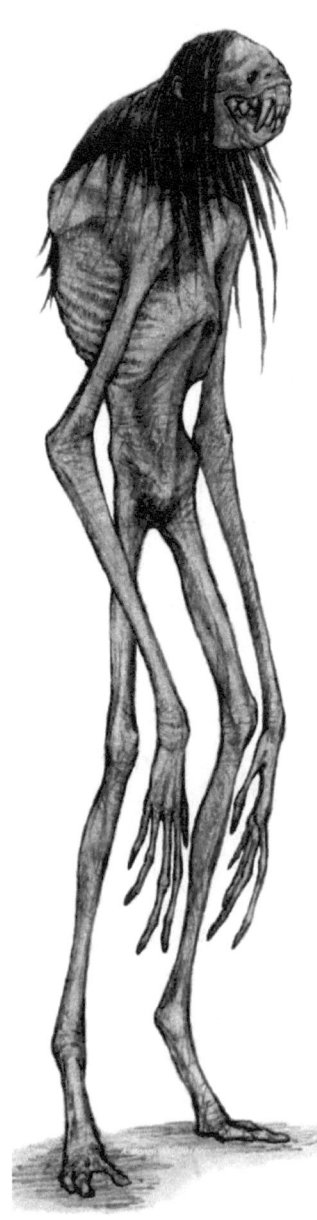

Artwork by
Aleksei Monzhalei

habit the snowman, using its man-like form as a gateway into the physical realm. This is somewhat similar to a tradition among the Pennsylvania Dutch where scarecrows (*Butzemenn*) must be burned before Halloween or risk being inhabited by malevolent spirits.

Perhaps because of the association with ice, wendigo monsters also have a supernatural affinity with water in general. This is not surprising, as most malevolent spirits in Native cosmology have a connection to water, like the Great Lynx (*Mishipeshu*), or Underwater Panther. Bodies of water are believed to be entry points to the Underworld. Lake Superior is believed to be the home of Mishipeshu. Lakes are naturally mysterious places, as so much lies unseen beneath their surface. Wendigos are said to be able to swim great distances and at amazing speed. In some tales wendigos are able to breathe underwater and live at the bottom of lakes, like Lake Windigo on Star Island in Minnesota, where there are tales of people finding holes in the ice with large footprints walking *away* from the hole, as if something had crawled *out* of the lake. Yet other stories describe wendigos walking on open water as if it were solid ground.

Wail of the Wendigo:
One of the most feared aspects of the wendigo is its terrible cry or howling wail. In many written accounts and oral narratives this is the first warning that a wendigo is approaching. It is often described as a keening high-pitched wail, or whistle, that is carried on the wind. In other tales wendigos make a bellowing sound that shakes the ground, sending entire villages into a panic. There are many accounts of a wendigo's wail causing paralysis to varying degrees. Victims are described as "frozen with fear" and slow to make a hasty retreat. In other cases, it is far more literal, creating a physical paralysis. People are frozen in their tracks, or rendered unconscious, making it easy for a wendigo to snatch up and devour its victims. Canadian anthropologist Diamond Jennes (1886-1969) recorded tales of wendigos and their powers. On the wendigo's howl he writes, "Its breathing is like the whistle of a train, audible for miles; and its shouting weakens the limbs of the Indian it pursues."

Transformation:
Another feature of the wendigo legend that makes it so fascinating is the creature's ability to take on varied forms—a shapeshifter, as many of the legends claim. Transformation is a common theme in many wendigo stories. Tales indicate they can control their size. They can "swell up" or "get big" if they are on a rampage, while at other times they can shrink down to normal human size. They also have the ability to transform into other animals, like owls.

In wendigo country owls are viewed with suspicion and dread, as it is believed they could be a wendigo in disguise or a feathered spy under a wendigo's control. Like the porcupine, they are one of the wendigo's creatures. In his paper "The Windigo in the Material World" Robert A. Brightman explores the connection between owls and wendigos, noting that both are formidable predators, and the piercing impassive stare of an owl is similar to the cold-blooded gaze of a wendigo. In fact, the proto-Algonkian word for wendigo, *wi-nteko-wa,* means owl among the Meskwaki, Miami-Illinois, and Cheyenne tribes. Belief that owls (or their eerie night-time calls) are omens of doom is a common feature in folklore from the American Southwest to the Subarctic. In Appalachian Mountain folklore the call of a screech owl is often interpreted as meaning someone will soon die. If an owl is heard hooting during the daytime (very unusual for owls) it means bad luck, or that witchcraft is afoot.

Harbinger of Misfortune:
In northern Minnesota and the Lake of the Woods region the figure of the wendigo has taken on an ominous role as a harbinger of doom. It's possible the belief stems from their connection to owls. Throughout the region wendigos are seen as something more spectral than physical, like a winter wraith. A sighting is considered a very bad omen, usually indicating that someone in the area will soon die. Usually the danger it presents is not through physical attack but as a messenger of ill portent. It functions much like the Irish banshee, phantom black dogs, the Mothman of Point Pleasant West Virginia, or Detroit's Nain Rouge, where appearances precede disaster and death.

Moss Eaters:
Moss and lichens are a recurring feature in wendigo lore, particularly when in their monstrous form. In some Cree folktales wendigos have the power to control moss, as in the tale "The Moss Falls Windigo." In the tale the wendigo is able to make moss grow all over its surroundings and even use it as a snare to capture and envelop unsuspecting victims. In this case moss could be seen symbolically as a spreading pestilence that clings to things and parasitically feeds off whatever it comes in contact with. Its parasitic nature is analogous to the wendigo spirit by the way it possesses and clings to victims, devouring their minds, and slowly encasing their hearts in ice.

While wendigos always prefer human flesh, they are sometimes omnivorous out of necessity. When humans are not available their hunger will drive them to eat almost anything, including meager sources of nourishment, like moss and lichens. In fact, a common name for wendigo is "Moss Eater." Sometimes when a person was suspected of being in the process of "going wendigo" their teeth were checked for bits of moss.

One species, a leather-like lichen called "smooth rock tripe" (*Umbilicaria mammulata*), is so linked to tales of wendigos that some tribes call it "windigo wakon" (wendigo cabbage). Explorers Radisson and Groseilliers described it as tasting horrible and having a glue-like consistency. The French called it *tripe de roche*, meaning literally "rock guts." It's very bitter and considered a last resort starvation food, as you have to be very desperate to eat it. It will make you feel full, but it doesn't provide much nutrition. It also has to be soaked and boiled several times to remove acids and render it edible. One is likely to expend more calories preparing it than they would likely receive from it. In the winter of 1777, George Washington's men filled their bellies with it at Valley Forge. It kept them alive, but they didn't thrive. If not prepared properly it can cause extreme bowel issues, nausea, and allergy symptoms.

It's possible that some cases of wendigo sickness reports of "swelling up" and loss of appetite for normal food could have been a reaction to eating unprepared moss and lichens. Furthermore, it's also possible that allergic reactions to toxins contained within rock tripe may lead to a state of delirium, causing victims (and witnesses) to believe someone was going wendigo. A possible nutritional explanation for wendigo symptoms is explored in Vivian J. Rohrl's paper, "A Nutritional Factor in Windigo Psychosis," where she notes that many psychiatric diseases are highly influenced by diet. It's worth restating that one of the main treatments for wendigo possession is the ingestion of melted fat, usually bear grease. Rohrl notes, "Bear fat might well contain some essential elements ... or it might restore normal blood sugar levels if one assumes acute windigo. It can occur during a hypoglycemic episode." In fact, wendigo symptoms often mirror symptoms of hypoglycemia (low blood sugar, which can be caused by starvation). Symptoms include shakiness, dizziness, sweating, hunger, irritability or moodiness, anxiety or nervousness, and headache. When someone is in a state of starvation, one of the best things for them is fat, which is very high in calories, fatty acids, and B vitamins. It's a super-fuel for restoring energy. Bear grease in particular may contain large amounts of other important vitamins, like vitamin C, derived from the bear's omnivorous diet, including berries.

Nutritional deficiency may be a contributing factor to psychosis and cannibalism, but it is not necessarily a singular cause. Many thousands of people worldwide experience starvation and nutritional issues, but fortunately it doesn't drive them to eat their own family members. Therefore we must view this information within a broader cultural context: that is, a culture that routinely experiences winter isolation and where the fear of "going wendigo" is a deep-rooted part of their belief system and an ever-present concern each winter—an uncommon, though by no means rare, feature of their society.

Tall Monsters or Tall Tales?

Stories of wendigo giants are often regarded as something of the distant past. By the mid-twentieth century, anthropologists found that stories of the cannibal giant had receded from the consciousness of many tribes. They had only vague memories about the mythic monster; it was always "far away and long ago." In the early 1940s anthropologist Horace Beck was told by Cree and Ojibwe informants that the wendigo was seldom seen and had withdrawn to the north. By the 1970s it was believed among some tribes that the last wendigo had been run over by a train around 1962. As the story goes, "The Wittiko was extremely hungry, having been deprived of human flesh for a long time. In desperation, he decided to stop the Canadian National Railroad train on the run from The Pas to Churchill and to eat the passengers. He stood on the tracks before the approaching train and attempted to paralyze the locomotive engineer and crew, and to stop the train by his terrifying appearance and superhuman power. His power was inadequate, and he was run over and killed." If one is to adhere strictly to the lore, it would be assumed the train's wheels severed the wendigo's head from its body (one of the ways to truly kill a wendigo).

We know that a sizable portion of wendigo lore is rooted in reality, as we can point to over three hundred years of court transcripts, police records, journal entries, and other documents clearly describing firsthand accounts of unfortunate people going mad, claiming to be possessed by the wendigo, and murdering and eating their victims. We know that cannibals and wendigo syndrome were real, but were the monstrous giant cannibal wendigos ever real? *Are* they real? As we mention in the Introduction to this book, the purpose of this book is not to determine whether or not wendigo monsters are physically real or not. We are not pushing the idea that wendigos are some kind of undiscovered "cryptid" lurking in the subarctic wilderness, nor are we advocating the idea that wendigos are merely colorful bits of Northwoods folklore. It would be more than a bit arrogant and presumptuous for authors who are separated both culturally, and by a few centuries, to determine what is "real" or not for those who experienced wendigo phenomena. Instead, we chose to present historical documentation and traditional narratives from varied groups so that readers can determine for themselves what they believe is "real."

It's easy to dismiss the monstrous giant aspect of the legend as "tall tales" akin to lumberjack legends of hoop-snakes, fur-bearing trout, or jackalopes. We know that a fair amount of wendigo stories definitely fall into the category of mythic fables, often with titles like, "The Weasel and the Wendigo," or stories crafted to make an etiological point such as, "How the Birch Tree Got Its Marks." Most of these are immediately recognizable by the inclusion of talking animals and contests of strength and heroism. Others are not as clearly fictitious and do not seem to have an obvious lesson to teach, other than a warning. What they all agree on is that a wendigo is something inhuman; either it never was (like an undying relic from a previous age before the arrival of Man), or if it was once a person, it is now completely devoid of all humanity and reason. It exists at the same level as other predators of the wilderness, albeit far more powerfully.

Anthropologist Richard J. Preston suggests that, unlike normal humans, wendigos are seen as feral predators. They can live unprotected in a harsh physical environment, easily find food, and withstand isolation and ostracism. Preston writes, "Witiko, while powerful and threatening to humans, is fundamentally another kind of creature with correspondingly different characteristics of competence. Witiko is a human transformed into a beast not only because he has dominated and eaten his family, but also because he lives on—with the kinds of competencies that are characteristic of non-human carnivores."

While researching this project we examined hundreds of wendigo stories spanning more than three centuries. Many of the earlier tales are narratives from Native informants recorded by white trappers, missionaries, and explorers. The result is that many of the stories are filtered through a Western lens by individuals who had poor understanding of Algonkian cosmology. It is easy to detect elements of cultural bias and subtle (and sometimes not-so-subtle) racial bias in most accounts. In numerous accounts indigenous people were described as "devil worshipers," "superstitious heathens," or "ignorant savages." Most chroniclers viewed stories of giant wendigos as nothing more than spooky campfire stories. The details of the tales were immediately dismissed as the product of wild imaginations and superstition. The irony that some of these same individuals were there to convince tribes of the real existence of an invisible and magical sky-god should not be lost on the reader. It shows a degree of disrespect and bias when stories are not taken at face value based on the racial and ethnic background of the informant. If generations of Algonkian people spanning an entire continent say giant cannibal wendigos were once real (and potentially still are?), why shouldn't we believe them? Anthropologist Robert A. Brightman echoes this sentiment in his paper "The Windigo in the Material World" when he says, "There remains a serious difficulty with the summary dismissal of all Algonquian testimony regarding the behavior of persons identified as windigo." Today, hundreds of rational people in North America claim to encounter sasquatch each year. In fact, around 20% of Americans believe that sasquatch is a real creature. If people are at least willing to entertain the possibility of the existence of something unknown, like sasquatch, why not the wendigo? Is it the relative obscurity of the legend, or is it cultural bias towards Native beliefs and traditions?

If giant wendigos are merely superstition, or part of mythic storytelling, what do we make of firsthand encounters recorded in modern times? One tale comes from Annie Moose, living in the Nelson House area in Manitoba's bush country. In 1979, at the amazing age of 112, she told the *Winnipeg Free Press* about an encounter she had with a wendigo near a place called Devil's Narrows about twenty-five miles south of Southern Indian Lake. She was gathering spruce boughs when she heard the sound of a large animal making its way through the forest. "A huge horrible-looking Wetego came out of the bush and headed for the children," Annie said. "That was the only Wetego I ever saw. It was bigger than the biggest man. It had a terrible-looking face—all hair with no lips. It made an awful groaning kind of sound." She rushed for her children and managed to get them away in a canoe before the windigo got them. "I paddled away as hard as I could while my husband stayed to drive the creature away," she said, adding, "From out in the Narrow we could see the Wetego waving a great big burning branch and setting fire to our camp. Finally, it moved on, but I can tell you it was very frightening—something you don't forget."

Another tale from the Nelson House area comes from Lionel Nicholas, an 83-year-old trapper. In a 1982 interview with the *Winnipeg Free Press* he recounted an encounter he had with a wendigo twenty years earlier. "It had hair that stood straight up, strange looking lips, and eyeballs that kept rolling around. It looked bigger than the biggest man I've ever seen and was very frightening," he recalled, adding, "I've heard of them wiping out whole settlements in the past. But I never actually saw anyone get killed or hurt."

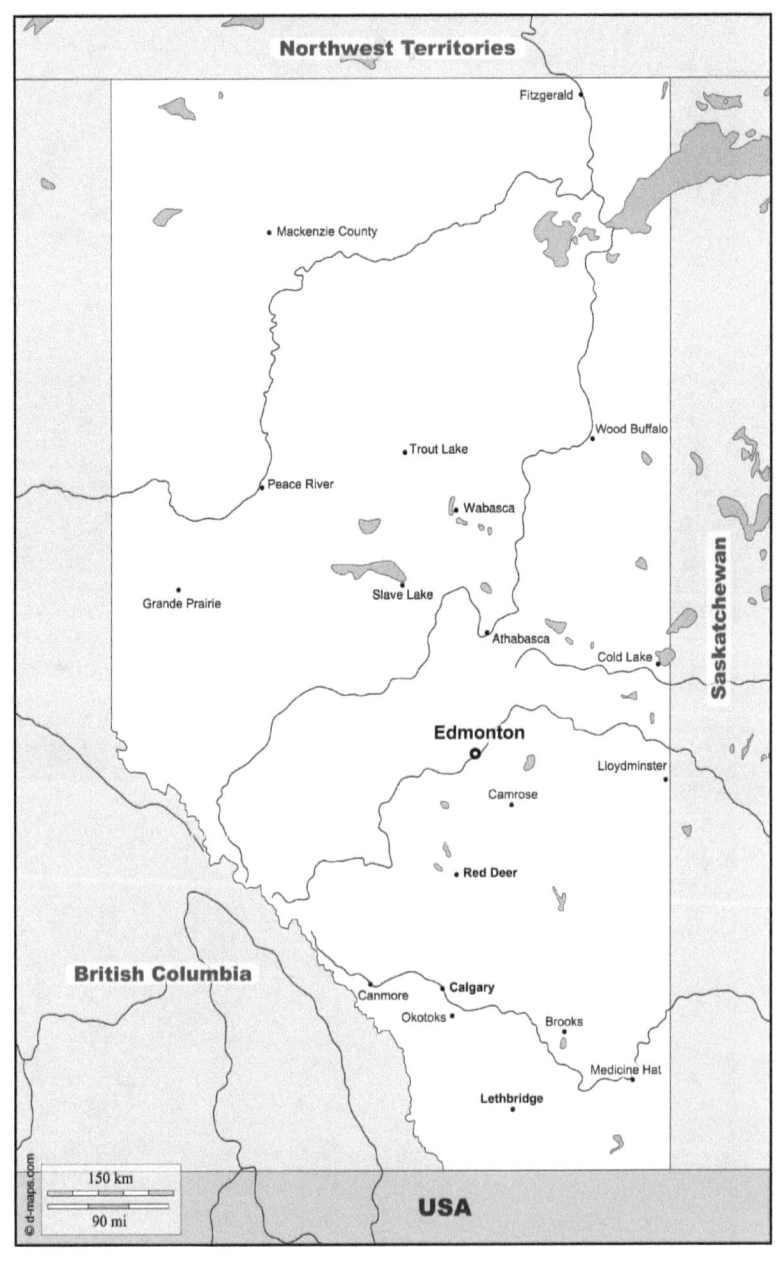

Map of Alberta and Athabasca District,
an area of numerous wendigo cases and reports

4
TERRITORY OF TERROR: ALBERTA, CANADA

If the wendigo had a focal point of belief, then the greater Slave Lake/Wabasca region would have certainly been the epicenter for the monster. Not only did Swift Runner (see next chapter) lurk in the region, but countless other gruesome killings and murders occurred throughout the entire area. I have always been a staunch believer in the idea that nothing allows you to appreciate a legend as much as actually being there and walking in the footsteps of the folklore. It was with this belief that Kevin and I traveled to Alberta in the winter of 2019 to grab a firsthand look at the wendigo hot zone in order to try to dig up some additional cases. We were a bit surprised at the treasure trove of wendigo stories that were waiting to be told, and keep in mind that these are simply the legends that got recorded. Imagine the possibly dozens and dozens of other wendigo cases that were regrettably lost to history. Even with these known cases, the mere fact that we intend to keep this book under 1,000 pages forced us to leave out a plethora of cases. The following wendigo stories are the most bizarre and puzzling of the Slave Lake/Wabasca region.

Marie Courterville Turns Wendigo

Marie Courterville's mental condition had rapidly deteriorated to the point where only death could deliver solace from the cannibalistic cravings that consumed her every ghastly thought and action. For several weeks, Marie had been caught in the inescapable grips of the wendigo, even as her loving family frantically tried to cleanse her of the evil spirit. It was the summer of 1887; Marie and her family were part of a larger encampment of Native peoples living

Approximate location of the original encampment
Photo by Authors

near the confluence of the Lesser Slave River and Lesser Slave Lake—just outside of Slave Lake, Alberta. Marie was relatively new to the Slave Lake area, having arrived just two summers prior with fervent hopes of escaping her tragic past. She had recently married Michael Courterville, the chief of the Lesser Slave Lake Indians. But this wasn't Marie's first marriage. According to an article in the *QuAppelle Vidette,* she had previously married a man from the Alexandre's band of Indians and the happy couple had seven children. Four years before arriving in Slave Lake, a dreadful fate began to curse Marie. First, her husband met his watery grave by drowning in the Pembina River. While she was still mourning the death of her husband, Marie's children began falling ill and dying as well. By the time she reached Slave Lake, only two of her seven children were still alive. The relocation to Slave Lake did nothing to disrupt her cursed fate, and soon her remaining two children joined their siblings in death. The unimaginable sorrow of losing her entire family was thought to be the impetus of her mental collapse. Whatever the cause of her illness, Marie was starting to turn into a raving

An article in the *Edmonton Bulletin* which covered Marie's death laid out the circumstances of her heartbreaking fall into insanity. Those living at Slave Lake began noticing something strange and odd about Marie's behavior, claiming, "she was very dull and would not eat" and "remained in this state for quite some time." Her mind wasn't the only thing changing; her body inexplicably began to swell, an odd condition that has accompanied several alleged wendigo cases as documented by researcher Nathan Carlson in his paper "Reviving Witiko (Windigo): An Ethnohistory of 'Cannibal Monsters' in the Athabasca District of Northern Alberta, 1878-1910."

Seeing his wife suffer from worsening mental and physical pains, Michael told her, "I think you are going to turn cannibal," to which Marie eerily replied, "It is to be that I aim to eat you. I like you all, but I am bound to eat you—kill me for I intend to eat you." Even with the dire death warning from his wife, Michael could not be persuaded to kill her, instead stating, "We can't kill you, we love you too much." Michael was not a fool, though, and as a precaution, he and his son Cecil hid all the weapons from Marie. Late at night, when Marie believed that those around her were sound asleep, she would frantically search for a weapon to kill her family. Eventually she was bound with heavy ropes as the two men tried everything they could to cure her; yet despite their best medicine, she continued to escape the ropes and threaten that she would kill and devour all of them. For over 20 days Marie suffered through some strange transformation of moaning while violently lashing out in fierce anger. Eventually her husband asked her if she was brave enough to leave this world—her reply was to roar like an animal. The men prayed and prayed, hoping to avoid the gruesome task of killing their loved one. The prayers failed, and the men feared that it was nearly too late to stop her from fully turning wendigo, so they grabbed two axes and smashed her with severe force on her head and breast. "When the deed was done the women and children around cried out with fright. The body kept moving for probably about an hour before she died."

A coffin was hastily constructed, and Marie was quickly buried that same evening. It is not known why her body was not burned, as fire was the more traditional means of disposing of a wendigo. Hearing of this killing, officers were sent to Slave Lake to arrest Michael and Cecil for the crime of murder. Neither man protested the arrest as they truly believed that they had done nothing wrong. In their eyes, they had saved their tribe from a cannibalistic wendigo who

Sawridge Cemetery
Marie's body was buried just outside of this cemetery.
Photo by Authors

would have undoubtedly devoured all of them. Not surprisingly, the law did not view it in the same manner and put the father and son on trial for murder. After a short deliberation, the jury found the two men guilty of manslaughter and both were sentenced to six years of hard labor.

It seems strange that so much emphasis was placed on this killing at a time when death from starvation and disease had fully engulfed the people around Slave Lake. An article in the *Plattsburgh Republican* detailed the carnage, writing, "Over 150 died last month from measles, and as the fisheries have failed, and the rabbits and lynx have deserted the country, they have no means of subsistence." In just one month over 150 people met their end, making it even more amazing that putting one severely ill person out of their misery would even echo through the death storm that was decimating Slave Lake.

Fast forward to December 2019 as Kevin and I stand at the site of the old Indian encampment along the mouth of the Lesser Slave Lake. The exact whereabouts of Marie's grave has been lost to history. Most likely she rests somewhere near the Sawridge Cemetery that sits beside the old encampment site. The heavily neglected cemetery houses several marked graves of unknown First Peoples in the area. The fact that Marie's body was never burned is not lost on Kevin and me as we explore the area in search of any clues to the wendigo's final resting place. Little did we know at the time, but the idea that the spirit of a wendigo was still roaming the cemetery grounds would not be the weirdest tale we would encounter in the Slave Lake area.

The Giant Man-Eating Monster of Eating Creek Road
During our expedition, we were scheduled to meet up with Pearl Lorentzen, a reporter and photographer with Slave Lake's *Lakeside Leader* newspaper. We met her at a local coffee shop and as we

Eating Creek as it looks today (in winter)
Photo by Authors

chatted with her, it became apparent that Pearl was a wealth of information on the area, despite being a relatively new transplant to the area herself. After swapping stories and folklore about the whetigo (wendigo), Pearl told us about an interesting local legend involving a cannibalistic monster that once inhabited a place called Eating Creek Road (Mitsue Road). In fact, back in 1992, her editor, Joe McWilliams, had written a fascinating article on the legend. Armed with that article, we headed to the outskirts of Slave Lake to find Eating Creek Road. The legend goes something like this. Long ago, many native people had an encampment along Eating Creek, a small trickle of water that eventually joins Mitsue Creek (Mitsue means eating) and then goes on to Lesser Slave River. According to McWilliams's research, the early people of the area believed that a giant man-eating whetigo lived amongst them. The beast's hunger for human flesh was insatiable, forcing it to constantly devour any human prey it could locate. The creek quickly developed a gruesome reputation, prompting the Native people to warn white fur traders to visit the area at their own peril lest they be eaten by the monster.

For his article, McWilliams interviewed two long-time residents of Eating Creek Road—brothers Leo and William Giroux, who recalled hearing the grisly stories of the cannibal while growing up in the area. In their grandfather's time someone became a 'whetigo' and began killing and eating those foolish enough to remain near the creek. The brothers didn't know "exactly when, or where it happened, or who was involved, but were brought up believing the stories." To make matters worse, the brothers were often told that "no normal human power could prevail against the whetigo,"—the absolute last thing any kid wants to hear about monsters.

While the majority of people that were turning wendigo were destroyed before they were able to go on a full-blown killing rampage, this apparently was not the case at Eating Creek. While expanding on this gruesome idea, McWilliams wrote, "That wasn't so at Mit-sue, according to the stories parents passed on to their children in the area. The Giroux brothers, among many others, are convinced the Mitsue names were given because a whetigo actually went wild and ate people, perhaps many people in that neighborhood." As Kevin and I walked along the banks of Eating Creek, the brothers' words echoed in our heads. One didn't need a lot of creativity to imagine this place as it actually was the 1800s, and even though the brothers stated that they were "glad we don't have whetigo any-more," Kevin and I continued to heed the old warnings and kept a steady hand on our hatchets.

The Lesser Slave Lake Wendigo Rescue

In 1897, the March 15th edition of the *Edmonton Bulletin* told the incredible story of two young women on a desperate run for their lives. On February 1, four dog trains left White Fish Lake and ar-rived in Lesser Slave Lake with two young sisters who were thought to be turning wendigo. It all began several days prior when the young women "were taken with a sudden sickness which the In-dians call 'witikaw' or cannibal." Filled with dread over the belief that the women were going to turn into wendigos and eat everyone, the people of White Fish Lake sacrificed two dogs in order to cure the women. When the sacrifice failed to alleviate their sickness, it was feared that the two unidentified women would soon be put to death. "Four men watched over them for three nights. They could hardly hold them when they were taken with the fits." A decision was made to rush the women to Lesser Slave Lake where they would be safer from any attempts on their lives.

Once they arrived at Lesser Slave Lake the justice of the peace or-dered them to the Roman Catholic Mission for treatment. While at the mission the sisters "took a light supper and slept well." Mirac-ulously, by morning, the women were feeling a great deal better. Their father arrived and found them "talking, laughing, and enjoy-

The home of a giant man-eating wendigo
Photo by Authors

Slave Lake is filled with wendigo legends.
Photo by Authors

ing themselves." By the next day, under the constant care of The Rev. Desmarais, the women were even stronger, so much so that it was believed that they would soon be able to return to White Fish Lake. The newspaper rightly noted that by caring for the women Father Desmarais "will undoubtedly prevent murder, for they were nearly sure to be killed." Whatever cures or medicine was administered, it succeeded in preventing them from becoming a wendigo. Eventually the women made their way back to White Fish Lake and were reunited with their husbands.

The Trout Lake Tragedy
"A Wendigo Murdered by His Companions for Their Own Safety." That was the tantalizing headline of an article in the May 8, 1896, edition of the *Glenboro Gazette*. The article told the terrible tale of a man being killed in Trout Lake the previous winter. The victim's

name was Napanin, and various newspapers described him as a "fairly intelligent man, about 35 years of age," who provided well for his wife and children. Sometime in late January, Napanin set out from Wapisca (Wabasca). He was in good health and was joined by his wife and children as they headed to visit his father in Trout Lake. The easy travel did not last long. On the second night of their journey, his wife reported that "he acted strangely, saying that some strange animals were about to attack him." The identity of the strange animals was never disclosed; perhaps it was the wendigo or perhaps some other weird creatures—as the forests were chock-full of legendary monsters. Whatever strange animal it was, it was so disconcerting that his wife, fearing for her life, pushed for him to go on ahead of the rest of the family. Upon reaching Trout Lake, his troubling condition continued to deteriorate, and for the next 20 days he was plagued with fits of insanity that became increasingly

Slave Lake provided a life-saving refuge for the two sisters.
Photo by Authors

A 'WEHTIGO' MURDERED.

Canadian Indians at Trout Lake Kill an Insane Companion— News of the Tragedy.

The Trout Lake wendigo killing made international news

more frequent and violent. Not only was he suffering from mental changes, his body was said to have "swelled considerably and his lips were much puffed out" (again the swelling). In his sporadic moments of lucidity "he told his friends that he did not intend to hurt anyone, but that if they considered him dangerous they had better kill him." While his wife and baby were out visiting a neighbor, the decision to kill him was made. Sensing that something wasn't quite right, his wife rushed back to her husband's room just in time to hear the death dealing blows of the axe. Apparently, the four men in the room had previously tried to secure Napanin with ropes, only to discover him wriggling free. They struck him with four blows of an axe, due to the "belief among Indians that a bullet will not pierce a 'wendigo' or man-eater."

The body of the wendigo was quickly burned and buried. After being burned, a series of large trees were "felled over the grave to prevent the possibility of a re-appearance of the 'wendigo.'" Such was the fear that the wendigo would rise up from death that any and all measures of finality were implemented. The four men responsible for Napanin's death, and many others in the tribe, strongly believed that his killing was "justified on the ground that unless he was killed he would have killed others."

Moostoos Turns Wendigo

One of the most infamous wendigo cases occurred in the winter of 1899. It happened at Smoky River, a place near Lesser Slave Lake in Northern Alberta. The extraordinary case was covered in numerous newspapers around the world, including the *Winnipeg Tribune* which published the complete court confessions of one of the defendants—Napaysoosis (Napaysoosee)—as translated by George Gairdner. Here is his version of events:

The band, which consisted of 32 members, was camped together in two shacks and two tepees. The hardships of winter had not strained the friendship and camaraderie that existed among the members living so close together. Everything had been going well until a man named Moostoos, who was especially well liked by everyone, began telling folks that "he was afraid an evil spirit was getting the better of him and that he would turn Wehtiko." Plagued by fear, he added, "If I ever go wrong you had better kill me as I do not wish to destroy my children." Soon, sickness was plaguing several tribe members, including a man named Napaysis, and Moostoos, who were both brought to Entominahoo's tepee. Entominahoo was the chief medicine man of the tribe and Moostoos went to him to "join in the medicine-making and sorceries which were being practiced with a view to curing the sick men." These measures once again confirm the notion that the sick and ill among a tribe were not quickly disposed of just to make life easier for the rest of its members. Whatever rituals and rites that were performed, they did not come to the aid of Moostoos who now took on a frightening appearance as "his eyes were rolling and glittering and he seemed afraid to look anyone in the face, and he was all the time muttering to himself." It appeared as though the wendigo's icy spirit was starting to possess Moostoos as he was overheard saying, "I look on these children as young moose and long to eat them." The sudden viewing of loved ones as tasty game animals was one of the telltale signs of wendigo possession. Apparently, the wendigo's work was swift, as later that evening Moostoos looked "wilder and more dangerous than ever." As a last-ditch effort, a special medicine lodge was constructed and "the whole skill and power of all our sorceries was enlisted in the attempt to bring Moostoos back to reason...the singing of medicine songs, drumming and dancing were carried on from sundown to almost midnight." At first, the medicine seemed to be working as Moostoos lay quietly on the floor. Then, out of nowhere, Moostoos shouted out, "This night you will all die" as his eyes again began to roll in his head; and as his body thrashed about, he continued, "If I get up, I will kill you all tonight." Then, springing to his feet with alarming speed Moostoos shouted "I will kill you all, I will not leave one alive." Perhaps realizing that the wendigo was already fatally embedded into Moostoos, Entominahoo whispered, "It's no use, I can do no more, do your best to hold him." Several people struggled to restrain Moostoos as he began whipping his head back and forth, grinding his teeth, and attempting to bite and tear at people as though he were a rabid wild animal.

The entire room was filled with extraordinary fear; their worst nightmare had become reality, the dreaded wehtiko had fully arrived. A woman named Eliza "sprang to her feet, holding in her right hand a medicine belt and in her left an axe. Her hair was flying loose as she was dancing and singing. All of a sudden she ran round and thrashed Moostoos over the face and breast with this medicine bag several times." Finished with her blows, Eliza then handed the axe to a man named Chuckachunk who smashed it over Moostoos's head, splitting his skull. Napaysoosis (the defendant) then drove a knife into Moostoos's body and stuck the axe into his chest. Outside, a man named Payoo (the other defendant), "alarmed by the screams of fear from the women and calls of the men," entered the shack. He was handed an axe and without hesitation smashed it into the head of Moostoos. Needless to say, Moostoos was dead—very dead, but here is the most interesting part, when the court asked Napaysoosis what they did next, he replied, "We sat round the body

The grisly case made for sensational news

until daylight." Even though Moostoos was without a doubt dead, the tribe "expected him to rise up from the dead, and we wanted to kill him again if he tried to get up."

If you thought the killing was excessive and gruesome, wait until you hear what they did to the wendigo after it was dead. Napaysoosis's testimony provided us great insight into the belief system surrounding the wendigo. The court asked him what the tribe believed was wrong with Moostoos—to which he replied, "He was a Wehtik, and I know he had a lump of ice in his body causing the malady." Not convinced that a wendigo could be killed so easily, Napaysoosis and Payoo grabbed Moostoos's dead body and drove a stake through the axe hole in his chest, pinning him to the ground. When they pulled out the stake, they poured boiling hot tea into the wound to thaw the wendigo ice that had spread throughout the body. As the morning sunlight was setting in, Napaysoosis was joined by Entominahoo's wife. Neither of them was convinced that Moostoos was completely dead, so they tied his legs with chains and attached the chains to two pickets in the ground so that if "he came back to life again he could not get up and run after us." Surely, they had entirely surpassed their due diligence and could rest easy in the fact that the wendigo was finally dead—NOPE! Napaysoosis grabbed an axe and proceeded to cut off the head of Moostoos just to be "sure he was dead and in order that, even if he got up, he could not eat us." After all the multiple attacks and brutal violence, they simply left Moostoos's headless body tied up in the shack.

This is an especially odd case when you consider that only Napaysoosis and Payoo were brought to trial for the killing. Although Napaysoosis's version was the most widely circulated in the newspapers, it wasn't the only version of events. Several other tribal members testified to various versions of the events that best suited them. If Chukachuck was the first one to smash his axe into the head of Moostoos, how did he escape prosecution? Regardless of what really transpired in that medicine tent, only Payoo and Napaysoosis were charged. Nine different people testified at the trial, including Chuckachuck and Payoo, and after four hours of deliberations the jury convicted Napaysoosis of manslaughter and acquitted Payoo. Believing that the killing was done in self-defense, the judge gave Napaysoosis a slap on the wrist and sentenced him to two months of hard labor.

The Windigo Prophet

Fear of the wendigo was so ingrained into the belief system of the region that the smallest remark or story could set off an avalanche of terror and panic. That is exactly what transpired with the "Windigo Prophet" a man who claimed to have dreamt that a deadly wendigo would soon arrive in the area to devour everyone. He stated that the only way to survive this insidious monster was to become followers of his as only his powerful medicine could protect them from certain death.

The St. Martin's Chapel had been constructed along the shores of South Wabasca Lake in part to help eliminate these traditional superstitions from the native peoples who were camped along the lake. For weeks on end the people in Wabasca would huddle in dread simply on a rumor that a wendigo was approaching—often refusing to leave to hunt, fish, or gather food. Even the deadly consequences of starvation weren't powerful enough to dislodge people from the safety of their dwellings. When faced with family members who were turning wendigo, many turned to the church for assistance. Legend tells that a visiting St. Martin's priest, Father Dupe, was able to cure a wendigo during his time in Wabasca, but no specific details accompany the legend.

While Kevin and I explored the grounds of St Martin's Parish we quickly realized the importance of the mission's proximity to the encampment of the native people. Being so close to the lake and the tribe allowed the mission to truly be hands-on in its effort to eradicate the wendigo belief. One doesn't need a highly formed imagination to picture the place as it was in the 1800s when the wendigo drama was unfolding.

One of the most infamous legends of Wabasca was said to have taken place during the late 1800s when a local man turned wendigo. Not wanting to sit by and wait for the man to devour the entire town, several men stormed the wendigo's cabin and shot him to death. For good measure, the wendigo's body was then staked into the ground while its cabin was burned down. Although there is some debate as to whether this case was merely an amalgamation of other regional cases, while in Wabasca, Kevin and I spoke with a younger bartender who informed us that the legend she often heard was that years ago a man went crazy and turned wendigo. The townsfolk chopped up his body and buried pieces of him at the four corners of the town in order to disperse his body, lest he try to return from the grave and seek revenge. Perhaps she was referencing the case of the same wendigo. Yet with all the wendigo fear that was paralyzing the community at that time, it certainly could have been two completely separate wendigo incidents.

On our research expedition to Wabasca, Kevin and I were able to dig up a lot of local folklore, yet we were a bit astounded to discover that the overwhelming majority of First Nation people we talked with had absolutely no idea about the "witiko" legend. It wasn't that they didn't have any personal stories or tales of the wendigo, they simply had never even heard of the creature. We spent some time talking with one older woman who was a life-long resident of Wabasca who informed us that the creature seemed to be a relic from her grandmother's time, and she hadn't given it much consideration as a modern legend.

Luckily, we were able to talk with several people who were familiar with the creature; usually their stories were generic tales of the monster that fell into the general myth-like tales, more allegorical than actual encounters with the wendigo. Yet these tales filled us with hope, knowing that the wendigo legend continues to lurk in the darker recesses of the mind. Upon leaving the area, we both felt that

St. Martin's Chapel as it looked in the 1800s

we had merely scratched the surface of Wabasca's lore and legends, a belief that will undoubtedly lure us back to the area for further digging.

St. Martin's Chapel as it is today
Photo by Authors

General location of the original native encampment
Photo by Authors

The Wendigo Lives On

After exploring and researching the Slave Lake/ Wabasca/ Athabasca regions of Alberta, Kevin and I came away with profound respect for the land. Being from the Northwoods of Wisconsin and having traveled through various far flung parts of Canada, and many of the world's other isolated places, we thought that we were fully acquainted with wild places. Yet there is something different, something unique, something primeval, about the wilds of Alberta that is hard to fully appreciate without actually being immersed in it. We felt as though we had merely cracked the surface of the wendigo lore that this region possesses; and as we openly wondered to each other about how much amazing wendigo lore had been forever lost to history, we were convinced that we were merely three or four generations too late to collect the purest and deepest roots of the legend. Our melancholy from being so tantalizingly close to that research window was lifted by those individuals we met on our journey, individuals for whom the wendigo legend was not relegated to the trash bin of history. For them, they will continue to share the legends, swap stories, and dig up more history to ensure that future generations will have the same opportunity to be terrorized by the wendigo as we do.

5

CANNIBALISTIC CHAOS: THE GRUESOME TALE OF SWIFT RUNNER

Chances are that if someone has even a cursory knowledge of wendigo lore, they have heard of the case of Swift Runner. He is perhaps the most infamous and widely-known case of a person turning wendigo. Yet most of this awareness is just at the periphery of the legend. The general public may know the basics—he killed and ate his family—but most are unaware of the gruesome and intricate details that make this case so puzzling, repulsive, and emotional.

The Indian Who Ate His Family.

The gruesome tale of Swift Runner is not for the faint of heart

Over the 15 years that I have been researching Swift Runner, I have spent countless hours trying to gain further insight into the mindset that forced him to commit these dastardly deeds. I have dug up any reference to the case I could find; I appeared on numerous TV shows talking about him and his actions; I even appeared in a wendigo based video game (an interview with me about Swift Runner pops up as a bonus to those who beat Until Dawn). However, it wasn't until 2019 that I finally had the opportunity to personally visit the sites where he lived, loved, murdered, and died. I have to say that I wasn't quite prepared for the emotional wallop that the trip would unleash.

Over the last two and a half decades I have visited countless places where individuals have done abhorrent things. I spent time at "Death Curve" in Illinois where Mrs. Markham took an axe and killed all seven of her children before dousing herself with oil and setting her house ablaze. I wandered along the farmland where Ed Gein dug up the bodies of dead women, turning their skin into grotesque lampshades and furniture for his home. I researched serial killers, mobsters, untimely deaths, and suicides, all the while thinking I had become overly immune to heinous acts.

I am writing this chapter's introduction as Kevin and I sit in our hotel just down the road from where Swift Runner was executed. We have spent the past few days retracing the story of Swift Runner as we bounce from one legend-cursed location to another. I wanted to commit my thoughts to paper while I am still immersed in Swift Runner's world. So why has Swift Runner provoked such an emotional response? ...well, you'll see....

Although dozens and dozens of newspapers throughout the world covered Swift Runner's sensational crimes, arrest, and trial, not one of them provided a clear narrative of what actually happened. The facts of the case varied widely from one news source to another. Frustratingly, the press couldn't agree on much of anything regarding Swift Runner. Even the most basic details of how many children he had ranged from 3 to 7. In some versions he was said to be accompanied by his mother and brother, in other versions they were his in-laws. The discrepancies go on and on and on. I will discuss many of the inaccuracies as we go along. After years spent struggling to sort fact from fiction, here is what we believe is the most accurate account of Swift Runner.

The History:
Swift Runner (*Kakisikutchin*) (Kaki-si-ku-chin) was a Cree Indian living in the heavily forested Athabasca region of Alberta, Canada.

He was approximately 40 winters old and enjoyed his large family which consisted of his wife and their six children—the youngest being just an infant. In the winter of 1878, accompanied by his mother and brother, Swift Runner and his family were traveling to his winter trapping grounds in search of food. The long winter season started off fine, with Swift Runner being able to kill numerous game animals. But as the cold icy winter wore on, things took an unfortunate turn. Game was almost nonexistent, and their food reserves were long gone. Faced with the real threat of starvation, Swift Runner had no choice but to be constantly on the move in search of life saving sustenance.

A few months later, in the spring of 1879, Swift Runner stumbled into the mission at St. Albert telling a heartbreaking tale of having to helplessly watch as his entire family starved to death. He was no stranger to the people of the area. The *Winnipeg Free Press* noted that the Hudson's Bay officers considered him "a trustworthy and intelligent guide" who had previously worked with the authorities numerous times in the past—even if his fondness for whiskey had long ago spoiled his guiding opportunities. Yet even his once good name could not dispel the immediate suspicions that were raised as to the credulity of his peculiar tale. His story simply did not add up. For one thing, Swift Runner did not appear emaciated as though he had just weathered starvation or any near-death scenario. In fact, his towering six-foot-three fame was filled out at over 200 pounds. If anything, he looked healthier than ever. Eventually the Mounted Police were summoned, and they persuaded Swift Runner to escort them back to his winter quarters so they could examine his family remains and corroborate his story.

A search party was organized to lead the shackled Swift Runner back to his winter camp. In his highly stylized book on Swift Runner's life, author Colin Thomson told of Swift Runner's understandable hesitation to lead the authorities back to his winter

A chapel at St. Albert's mission as it looks today
Photo by Authors

quarters, knowing full well that the grisly evidence would expose his web of deceit. After several days of being led in circles, the guards, knowing "of the prisoner's love of 'muss-kee-wah-bwee' (alcohol to which a large quantity of plug tobacco was added)," decided to get Swift Runner drunk in hopes that his intoxication would loosen his lips. Apparently, the alcohol did the trick and they soon discovered the virtual graveyard left behind in Swift Runner's wake. They had walked into a scene straight out of a horror movie. The bones and skulls of his family were scattered about everywhere. Several of the bones had been snapped in half with the marrow having been sucked out. Kettles were caked with the boiled remains of human flesh. Swift Runner was said to have casually walked over and picked up a skull by putting his fingers through the eye socket. Many newspapers, including the *Daily British Whig* claimed Swift Runner nonchalantly said, "this is my wife," while holding the skull, while many other newspapers including the *Victoria Daily British Colonist* claimed that he remarked "this is my mother." Regardless of whose skull it was, the men had seen enough and quickly gathered as much of the evidence as they could load up— the rest they buried.

The Confession:
So what exactly did happen during those deadly winter months? Perhaps, the most accurate account stems from an article in the February 9, 1880, edition of the *Saskatchewan Herald*, which was written by Reverend Father Hippolyte Leduc, a French Catholic Missionary based in St. Albert who ministered to Swift Runner during his final days. This was the alleged confession Swift Runner gave to Father Leduc:

> We were camped in the woods about eighty miles from here. In the beginning of winter, we had not much to suffer. I killed many moose and five or six bears; but about the middle of February, I fell sick,

Swift Runner in shackles as he awaited trial
Image courtesy of Archives and Special Collections,
University of Calgary

Kevin Lee Nelson recreates the Swift Runner photo
next to the reconstructed fort.
Photo by Authors

and to complete our misfortune those with me could find nothing to shoot. We had soon to kill our dogs and lived on their flesh while it lasted. Having recovered a little from my sickness I traveled to a post of the Hudson's Bay Company, on the Athabasca river and was assisted by the officer in charge and returned to my camp with a small amount of provisions. That did not last us long. We all-that is my mother, wife, and six children (3 boys and 3 girls), besides my brother and I—began to feel the pangs of hunger. My brother made up his mind to start with my mother in search of some game. I remained alone with my family. Starvation became worse and worse. For many days we had nothing to eat. I advised my wife to start with the children and follow on the snow the tracks of my mother and brother, who perhaps had been lucky enough to kill a moose or bear since they left us. For my part, though weak, I hoped that remaining alone I could support my life with my gun. All my family left me with the exception of a little boy, 10 years of age, who obstinately refused to leave me.

I remained many days with my boy without finding any game, and consequently without having a mouthful to eat. One morning I got up early. Suddenly an abominable thought crossed my mind. My son was lying down close to the fire, fast asleep. Pushed by the evil spirit I took my gun and pointed it at the poor innocent, while turning my head away, I shot him. The ball entered the top of his skull. Still he breathed. I began to cry' but what was the use? Impossible now to recall him to life. I then took my knife and sunk it twice into his side. Alas!

He still breathed, and I picked up a stick and killed him with it. I then satisfied my hunger by eating some of his flesh, and lived on it for some days, extracting even the marrow from the bones.

Some days afterwards, in wandering through the woods, unfortunately I met my wife and children. I said to them that my son had died of starvation, but I remarked immediately that they suspected the frightful reality. They then told me that they had not seen either my mother or brother. No doubt both have died of starvation, otherwise they would have been heard of, as it is now seven months since then. Three days after joining my family the oldest of my boys died. We dug a grave with an axe and buried him. We were then reduced to boil some pieces of our leather tent, our shoes, and buffalo robes, in order to keep ourselves alive.

I discovered soon that my family wanted to leave me for fear of meeting the same fate as my boy. One morning I got up early, and I didn't know why—I was mad. It seems to me that all the devils had entered my heart. My wife and children were asleep around me. Pushed by the evil spirit, I took my gun, and placing the muzzle against her chest, shot her. I then without any delay took my hatchet and massacred my three little girls. There was now but one little boy, seven years old, surviving. I awoke him and told him to melt some snow for water at once. The poor child was too much weakened by long fasting to make any reflection on the frightful spectacle under his eyes. I took the bodies of my little girls and cut them up. I did the same with the corpse of my wife. I broke the skulls and took out the brains and broke up the bones in order to get the marrow. My little son and I lived for seven or eight days on the flesh—I eating the flesh of my wife and children, and he the flesh of his mother and sisters.

At length I left there all the bones and started with the last of my family. Snow began to melt. Spring had commenced. Ducks arrived and flew everyday around us, and I could find enough to live on: but I felt reluctant to see people. I then told my son that after some days we would meet people; they will know very soon that I am a murderer, and they will certainly make me die. As to you, there is no fear; say all you know; no harm will be done to you. One day I killed many ducks. I was a few miles from Egg Lake, where some relations of mine lived. I was sitting at the campfire, when I told my son to go and fetch something five or six paces off. At that moment the devil suddenly took possession of my soul; and in order to live longer far from people, and to put out of the way the only witness to my crimes I seized my gun and killed the last of my children, and ate him as I did the others.

Just take a moment to let the brutal inhumaneness of these last few paragraphs settle in…Okay, several things really popped out to me while reading this confession. First, I find it very interesting that Swift Runner denied that he had murdered his mother and brother since it was widely reported in nearly every newspaper account of the killings. Yet, at this point he had no reason to lie; the confession of killing his children was more than adequate to ensure his death, hiding two more murders would have served him no real purpose

Father Hippolyte Leduc

outside of absolving him of additional guilt, a guilt that he in no way exhibited anyway. Based on this, I am inclined to believe that his mother and brother truly did just simply walk away from camp and probably succumb to starvation as well. Regardless of the true details, Swift Runner is regularly implicated in their deaths. One of most commonly repeated stories tells of Swift Runner making the joke that his mother-in-law tasted a bit tough (although it was his mother who was with him). When officers found the grave of his oldest son, who Swift Runner had claimed died of starvation, they noticed tell-tale signs of malnourishment on the boy's emaciated corpse, adding further evidence that Swift Runner was being truthful about his deeds.

For decades, researchers and scholars have argued back and forth regarding whether or not Swift Runner's actions were committed in a famine context. Did the desperation of food scarcity cause Swift Runner to commit such heinous acts? For me, the answer is both yes and no. From his confession it is plain to see that midway through winter the lack of any nourishment seemed to be the culprit propelling him into deadly action. However, once spring arrived and the ducks had returned, food was apparently plentiful and there

The remains of Swift Runner's family were gathered for evidence.
Image courtesy of Archives and Special Collections,
University of Calgary

should have been no hunger related reason for Swift Runner to kill and consume his last remaining son. Yes, he certainly would have wanted to eliminate the only remaining witness to his crimes, but why also consume him? Perhaps, the answer lies in the evil spirit (wendigo) that he believed was inhabiting him. The compulsion to kill and eat his son may have been too powerful to resist, regardless of the other available food options.

Researchers have also speculated on why Swift Runner didn't simply hike to a trading company and ask for provisions. Scholar after scholar has brought up the fact that Swift Runner was within 25 miles of a Hudson's Bay camp and he could have easily hiked there anytime he wished, but he decidedly chose not to. Not only is this exactly what he did earlier in the season, but I feel that many people oversimplify and underestimate the monumental physical and mental task that this excursion would entail. As Kevin and I were standing in the general area of Swift Runner's winter camp we were awestruck by the remoteness of the area. Nearly 140 years later, the forests remained thick with underbrush and were nearly impenetrable and unruly. The notion that a 25-plus mile hike through several feet of snow and ice, battling snow drifts and howling winds in the sub-zero temperatures, would have merely been a walk in the park is preposterous. Anyone who has ever trudged through deep snow can appreciate the grueling exertion that is required to make the slightest progress. Throw in Swift Runner's severely weakened state due to months of malnourishment, and the fort may as well have been twenty-five million miles away. Of course, this is assuming that the wendigo hadn't already completely possessed him, making the whole question moot.

It is also in the mentioning of an evil spirit taking over his mind, body, and soul that we start to witness Swift Runner's shifting of blame for his actions. While he saw himself as the helpless victim under possession of a powerful witiko (wendigo), non-indigenous researchers viewed it as a clear sign he was suffering from a dissociative disorder, disconnecting himself from his thoughts, actions, and surroundings. Swift Runner also displays possible signs of paranoia in believing that his wife immediately suspected him of killing their son, even though starvation would have been the more likely and believable cause of death. For those who dispel the wendigo as purely fantasy, this only adds more credence to the general idea that mental illness, not a cannibalistic ice monster, was the root cause of his actions. If we view his words through the lens of being possessed by the wendigo, he is all but clueless as to why he committed the killings, as though he were in some state of mental fog or confusion. If you subscribe to the wendigo legend, you could understand that the beast was so powerful and all-consuming that Swift Runner was nothing more than a puppet, controlled by the insatiable hunger for human flesh. These conflicting theories are hashed out in greater detail in the Windigo Psychosis chapter, but for now we have a trial to attend.

The Trial:
On the 16th of August a court was held at Fort Saskatchewan. The proceedings were covered by the *Winnipeg Free Press,* and by all accounts it was a fair trial, the jury being comprised of six men, four of whom spoke Swift Runner's language (Cree). During his statement, Swift Runner once again detailed his guilt and re-told the ghastly details of his crimes. However, he also added, "I am going to tell the whole truth. I have done a good deal of wrong and for that reason I was backward at telling about it. I did not kill anybody's children but my own." This last statement provides us with another unique glimpse into the distorted thinking of Swift Runner, believing that his life should be spared because only he suffered the loss of family, no other children were harmed. As you can imagine, it didn't take long for the jury (20 minutes) to issue its verdict . . . Guilty! The execution was set for December 20th. In the meantime, the wendigo would remain jailed at the fort.

The Execution:

December 20th was a perfect day to kill a wendigo. Temperatures had plummeted to a bone-chilling -40 degrees as dozens of people gathered to witness the first hanging in the Canadian Northwest Territories. From the start, mishaps and blunders gave the hanging an almost comical tone. The execution had been scheduled for 7:30 a.m. and curious townsfolk and Native peoples had begun gathering hours earlier in order to witness the historical event. The *Savannah Morning News* reported that gallows had been built outside so Indians could see the event "but when officers and prisoner arrived at the spot, it was found that most of the scaffold had been used for firewood by the half-frozen crowd." As workers scrambled to rebuild the gallows, Swift Runner calmly warmed himself by the fire with the noose dangling around his neck as he enjoyed a final breakfast. The *Winnipeg Free Press* also commented on the haphazardness of the whole procedure, writing that the hangman "was very nervous, and when everything else was ready it turned out that he had no straps for pinioning his man." The hanging was once again delayed as the hangman ran to retrieve his tools of the trade. Looking to get the whole ordeal over with, Swift Runner told officers that if they gave him a tomahawk, he would do the job himself. Eventually the hangman returned, and the execution continued.

There was also a lot of confusion as to the means of execution. The First Nation people assumed that Swift Runner would be chopped into pieces. Again, the *Winnipeg Free Press* commented, writing "the Indians who never before saw or heard of death by hanging were anxious to know if it were a species of torture." Swift Runner had asked to be shot instead of hanged, but his request was refused. At approximately 10 a.m., "one of the police officers attempted to read a prayer, but his voice was drowned out by the jeers and shouts of the Indians." Finally, the signal was given, the trap fell, and with a drop of about 5 feet, the wendigo was dead.

Was There a Priest or Not?

Another sticking point was whether or not Swift Runner wanted a priest with him in his final moments. Almost universally, newspapers like the *Jackson Sentinel* reported that when offered a "black coat" (priest) he replied, "The white man has ruined me, and therefore I don't think their God could amount to much." In other versions it was the white man's whiskey that ruined him and therefore their God could not amount to much. This flies in the face of Father Leduc's version of events that told of Swift Runner converting to Christianity in the days before his execution, giving confession and asking the Almighty for forgiveness. Leduc claimed he was with Swift Runner to the very end, including being there at the gallows. Regardless, Leduc and several other priests did spend a considerable amount of time with Swift Runner as he was jailed at Fort Saskatchewan. We also have to consider that Leduc had both a personal and professional motive to embellish Swift Runner's apparent full-hearted conversion to the church. As a missionary, Father Leduc's main initiative would have been to convert the Native peoples to Christianity. To his credit, Father Leduc seemed genuinely concerned for the spiritual welfare of Swift Runner—both in this world, and the next, and sought to provide comfort, solace, and faith to the convicted cannibal. The confusion and discrepancies about a priest being present at the hanging could also have been another blatant attempt to cast Swift Runner as the wild ignorant savage stereotype—a stereotype that plagued many newspaper reports of the day.

What Happened to His Body?

The eternal fate of Swift Runner's body is also a matter of debate. Until now, the prevailing theory was that Swift Runner was unceremoniously buried at the Fort's Gaol (jail) Cemetery where the remains of unclaimed prisoners would be put to eternal rest. The city had kept detailed records of everyone who was buried in the cemetery. In the 1950s the Gaol Cemetery was relocated down the road

Kevin Lee Nelson at the grave site of Father Leduc
Photo by Authors

in order to make room for the construction of Highway 15 and all the records were lost. All of the graves in the current Gaol Cemetery are unidentified.

When we visited the historic Fort Saskatchewan museum, several staff expressed doubts that Swift Runner's remains are in the Gaol Cemetery. For one thing, the fort did not become an official jail until 1915, meaning that it was unlikely that the fort had a cemetery for its inmates 17 years before they even housed inmates. If Swift Runner was buried at the fort, it probably would have been in a much different location than other future inmates.

Several newspapers, including the *Winnipeg Free Press,* reported that once Swift Runner's body was cut down from the gallows it was "buried in the snow outside the fort." Since the ground would

Some believe that Swift Runner's remains were
transferred to the Gaol Cemetery.
Photo by Authors

have been completely frozen, the idea that he was quickly buried seems far-fetched. This theory is the one echoed by museum staff who had also heard that his body was wrapped up and hastily dumped outside the walls of the fort. There is also the possibility that his own people gathered the body and burned or buried it. The fear that he was a wendigo would have simultaneously forced people to keep their distance, yet at the same time there would have

We believe this is the most likely location
of Swift Runner's remains.
Photo by Authors

been a powerful need to properly dispose of his body to insure he was truly dead. I would have to concur with the museum staff that the most likely scenario was that Swift Runner was dumped somewhere on the fort grounds. Whether he was buried during the spring thaw is unknown.

While we were walking around the grounds of the historic fort, we dug up some interesting stories that may shed some additional light on the whereabouts of his body. While discussing the possible final resting place with some of the staff members, one of them told us that oftentimes while she is giving tours, people who believe they are psychic, especially those who are First Nation/Native, report sensing the spirit of Swift Runner lingering about at the historic site. Additionally, both tour goers and staff alike have seen strange apparitions moving about on the grounds. Those who are more open to the supernatural may see this as additional evidence that Swift Runner's body is indeed resting on the fort's ground.

Finality:
It was while I was standing in the snow-covered woods near Swift Runner's winter camp that the heinousness of this case truly hit me. As I have previously mentioned, I have spent years studying Swift Runner, but it wasn't until I walked the same land that he walked that the atrociousness of his actions fully sank in. For a long spell I sat staring off into the wilds trying to put myself into the shoes of his last remaining son. The same son who suffered the sight of his father's murderous metamorphosis into the wendigo. The same son who not only had to feast on his mother and sisters but had to deal with the unavoidable fact that the next victim would be him. Yet at the same time, the monster standing in front of this poor seven-year-old boy was his own flesh and blood father. Deep inside he had to have struggled with the question of how his main protector in this world could betray him in the most sinister way possible. It has taken me many weeks to shake the unnerving feeling that enveloped

me while sitting in those woods. And still on dark and quiet nights back here in Wisconsin I occasionally feel that icy coldness trying to creep back into my heart, and I think that perhaps the curse of the wendigo is truly eternal.

.

6

THE LAST WENDIGO HUNTER: THE LIFE AND DEATH OF JACK FIDDLER

Jack Fiddler (Zhauwuno-geezhigo-gaubow) seemed destined to become a wendigo hunter. His father, Chief Porcupine Standing Sideways, was widely known throughout the Sandy Lake region for being a powerful shaman who was capable of killing wendigos, and his arrival at the Sucker Clan was filled with mystery and intrigue. He was not born into the Sucker Clan, and in their wonderful book on the history of the Fiddlers and the Sucker Clan, *Killing the Shamen,* authors Thomas Fiddler (Jack's Grandson) and James Stevens tell a wonderful story of how Porcupine Standing Sideways came to be, "He was a personage who stepped from the other world into this one." He abruptly showed up as a young man, claiming, "They call me Porcupine Standing Sideways; I have lived before in this world, now I am here again." Sensing his powers, the tribe welcomed him into their clan. Although he was accompanied by his family, he would go on to father three more boys (Jack Fiddler, Joseph Fiddler and Peter Flett). At the time, Porcupine Standing Sideways had no idea that the wendigo would bring such devastating sorrow and turmoil to his family.

Eventually, Porcupine Standing Sideways would become Chief of the Sucker Clan. Thomas Fiddler wrote that in the time period Porcupine Standing Sideways was living, "people could kill each other with their curses," yet Porcupine Standing Sideways was "known for his invulnerability," often proudly boasting that no man could harm him through spells. This was also a time of incredible fear of the wendigo, as many believed the giant monster was actually living and lurking right in their midst. As a powerful medicine man, the responsibility of protecting the tribe from a murderous wendigo fell directly onto the shoulders of Porcupine Standing Sideways—and he did not disappoint. Thomas Fiddler tells of one such incident, writing, "They used to say that when a windigo was after some victims, people who had power would be drawn into a state when the windigo was nearby." One day his grandfather heard a loud thumping on the ground and sensed it was a deadly wendigo approaching. As the rest of the tribe ran terrified from the area, Porcupine Standing Sideways, armed with a knife, whip, and axe, bravely set out to confront the wendigo. "When he met this windigo, all of a sudden, the wind started blowing, clouds formed and trees bent to the ground like blades of grass blowing in the wind. Sounds like shots being fired were heard." However, it wasn't gunshots that were heard, it was the sharp cracking of the whip as the chief relentlessly attacked the wendigo. After each powerful snap of the whip the wendigo would touch at its bleeding head to ensure that it was still attached to its body. After some time, Porcupine Standing Sideways victoriously arrived back at camp—he had whipped the wendigo to death (a trick his son would use years later) and the monster's body was carried away. For a long time after this battle, it was said that when the snow was almost completely melted, thundering sounds could be heard at that exact spot of the battle due to the drops of wendigo blood that were spilled there during the fight.

In 1891, Porcupine Standing Sideways died and Jack Fiddler, who was thought to be approximately 60 winters in age, became the chief of the Sucker Tribe. It is not known exactly what previous experience he had with fighting the wendigo, we can only assume that by his age, he was already proficient in the ways of wendigo hunting, and his powerful lineage would serve him well in his own future battles with the monster. The white men knew his family as skillful fiddle players so they gave them the name "Fiddler." White people called him Jack Fiddler, but his own people knew him as He Who Stands in the Southern Sky.

Constable Parkinson along with prisoners Norman Rae,
Angus Rae, & Joseph Fiddler
Image courtesy of RCMP / Library

Just like his father, Jack Fiddler enjoyed a wide regional reputation that told of his curing abilities. Strangers often feared his shamanic powers which included an uncanny ability to communicate with forest animals. He was also considered a deadly opponent for any wendigo and all evil forces in general. Chief Thomas Fiddler expanded on Jack's powers, writing, "More important was Jack Fiddler's curing skills and his ability to call creatures for people's needs." Others claimed, "The reason he had such powers—to kill a windigo—is because he slept and dreamed. During these dreams, he was given the power to kill such an evil one. Not many people, but some people, have the ability to do such things." After defeating a wendigo, Jack would often drive stakes into the ground and pull the body right through them—before setting fire to the wendigo's bloody carcass.

Just how many wendigos Jack killed during his lifetime is unknown and under great debate. His grandson, Chief Thomas Fiddler, stated that "During his long life he said that he destroyed fourteen windigos." The *Winnipeg Tribune* and many other newspapers put the number near 20, while the *Waterloo Daily Courier* (among many others), reported that Jack had killed as many as 26 wendigos. In all likelihood, we will probably never know the true number of wendigos that Jack destroyed, but whether it was 14, 20, 26, or 200, it definitely places him as one of the most prolific wendigo killers in history.

Just as the tally of his killings will never be truly determined, we may also never know whether all the killings were those of people turning wendigo or that of the giant creature itself. Based on the rarity of encountering the giant cannibalistic version of the wendigo, we can speculate that the majority of Jack's killings came from those who had not fully transformed into a wendigo monster.

The one wendigo killing that caught the attention of the authorities happened in the fall of 1906. A young woman named Wahsakapee-quay fell ill and was rapidly becoming delirious (a sign of wendigo possession). She was brought to Jack Fiddler and his brother Joseph Pesequan/Fiddler (her father-in-law) due to their extraordinary ability to defeat a wendigo. Her groans of pain were loud and unrelenting, and her body was roiling in pain—something had to be done to end her suffering. It was quickly determined that in order to prevent her from turning into a wendigo, the young woman had to be killed. As several members of the tribe held her hands and legs, Jack and Joseph slipped a cotton covered cloth (string) around her neck and pulled until death was final. A hole was quickly dug and filled with wood and the dead woman's body was set ablaze, thus preventing the wendigo from returning.

Inside the courtroom of Joseph's trial
Image courtesy RCMP / Library and Archives Canada /
e003895324

In June of 1907, the authorities caught wind of this wendigo killing. Looking for an opportunity to exert more control over the Native peoples, and to stomp out what they believed was a barbaric tradition, the Mounted Police sent several officers to the Sucker Clan lands in order to make arrests. When the tribe was informed that Jack and Joseph were being arrested and would be brought to trial over one hundred miles away from their ancestral home, they were completely dumbfounded. Obviously, the officers could appreciate the remoteness of the area, an extremely isolated region where no medicine or medical care existed for hundreds of miles. The tribe passionately argued that they were simply putting their deathly ill family members out of their misery. They did not allow their animals and pets to suffer, so why would they allow their loved ones to waste away in agonizing pain, only to morph into a wendigo? Were they not simply doing the humane and compassionate thing? Was killing an alleged wendigo that different from sentencing people to the gallows? As you can imagine, the tribe was emotionally torn up about the arrests and openly cried over the perceived injustice. Regardless of their inability to fathom the officers' way of thinking, Jack and Joseph went peacefully to the Norway House to await trial for their crimes. From the onset, many non-Native people involved with the case expressed deep reservations about the brothers being arrested and tried over their cultural practices. Yes, they had indeed killed a woman, but it hadn't been conceived with malice or hatred, it was done out of fear and compassion. Legal experts further opined that the Fiddlers were completely unaware of the white man's ways and shouldn't be held to account for laws that were obviously so foreign to them.

Grainy 1907 newspaper photo - caption reads "The two R.N.W.M.P. officers J.A. O'Neil and W. Hashman, as they appeared when starting alone on their journey, 400 miles and return, to arrest and bring in the Indian murders. The figure to the left is O'Neil."

It is quite an understatement to say that the newspapers overly sensationalized this wendigo killing. Papers from around Canada and the U.S. were emblazoned with headlines reading "Devil Worship Among the Crees," "Wholesale Murder," "Indian Must Die," "To Stop Devil Worship," "Fiendish Work of Northern Indians," and "Murdered Daughter to Cast Out Devil," among countless others. Of course, many of the newspapers never failed to mention what they considered to be primitive and savage behavior, most equating it to an act of evil or devil worship. A few newspapers did comment on the remoteness of the area and its great distance from any hos-pital or medical assistance of any kind, stating that "many of them have never seen a white man."

The complex and nuanced legal arguments were all for naught, at least for Jack Fiddler. On September 30th, after being held prisoner for over 100 days, Jack leisurely walked into the forest during the daily morning fire-wood gathering expedition. By the time the pre-occupied Constable noticed that Jack was missing, it was already too late. Once in the woods, Jack had devised a way to forever free himself from captivity as he took off his assumption belt, slipped it around his neck, and attached the other end to a tree. His lifeless body was found lying on a rock with the large slip knot still tight around his neck. The official cause of death was suicide by strangulation. So ended the notorious life of the last wendigo hunter. Perhaps it was a fitting end that Jack left this world by the same manner of strangulation that he used to take the lives of so many wendigos.

Still convinced of the brothers' guilt, and more importantly the necessity for punishment, officers were not about to let a suicide thwart justice, so they trudged forward. The trial of Joseph Fiddler began on October 7, 1907. After a full day of testimony, the jury retired to discuss Joseph's fate. Immediately, it was obvious that the jury was extremely conflicted by the complexities of this case, which resulted in their inability to reach a verdict. Realizing the type of political pressure surrounding this case, the judge sent the jury back to their deliberations with instructions to work together in order to reach a verdict. The jury's apprehension stemmed from the fact that their only two options were to convict Joseph of murder or let him go scot-free, as no less severe alternatives to murder would be permitted. Eventually the jury returned a verdict of guilty; however, they did add a recommendation that mercy be shown to the defendant. The judge sentenced Joseph Fiddler to death by hanging. In January of 1908, a now very ill Joseph Fiddler was transferred to Stony Mountain where natural death finally caught him. The entire time Joseph was in captivity, those involved in the case petitioned for his release. Several letters requesting a full pardon were written on Joseph's behalf, some were even signed by a

Grainy 1907 newspaper photo - caption reads "From left to right , the group includes Chief John Pa-eja-quan and his nephew Jose, charged at Norway House with the murder of the chiefs stepdaughter, and two young members of the Fiddler tribe, Owl and Angus Rhea, held as eyewitnesses of the crime."

few of the men who served as jurors at his trial. In one last ironic twist, a few days prior to his death, Joseph had actually been pardoned for the crime, the official pardon arriving several days after he died.

In the first paragraph I mentioned that the family of Porcupine Standing Sideways, the famed wendigo hunter, would ultimately suffer the curse of the wendigo. Porcupine Standing Sideways had three sons, Jack Fiddler, Peter Flett, and Joseph Fiddler; all met their death due to their belief in the wendigo. As you just read, Jack and Joseph died after being arrested for killing a wendigo. While ill, Joseph pleaded with the authorities for his release, claiming that it was captivity itself that was causing his illness, and that if he were to be released to his people and his lands, he surely would recover. Peter Flett, the middle son, also fell victim to the wendigo curse. Chief Thomas Fiddler and James Stevens tell the tragic tale of Peter's death in their book, *Killing the Shamen*. It was 1894 when Peter and his family were traveling with many others near the west end of Caribou Lake. Peter suddenly fell ill and began exhibiting the signs of becoming a wendigo. Fearing that it was only a matter of time before Peter attempted to devour them all, the group quickly killed him. His body was burned to ashes in order to prevent his vengeful return. When all was said and done, the wendigo had taken the lives of all of Porcupine Standing Sideways's sons.

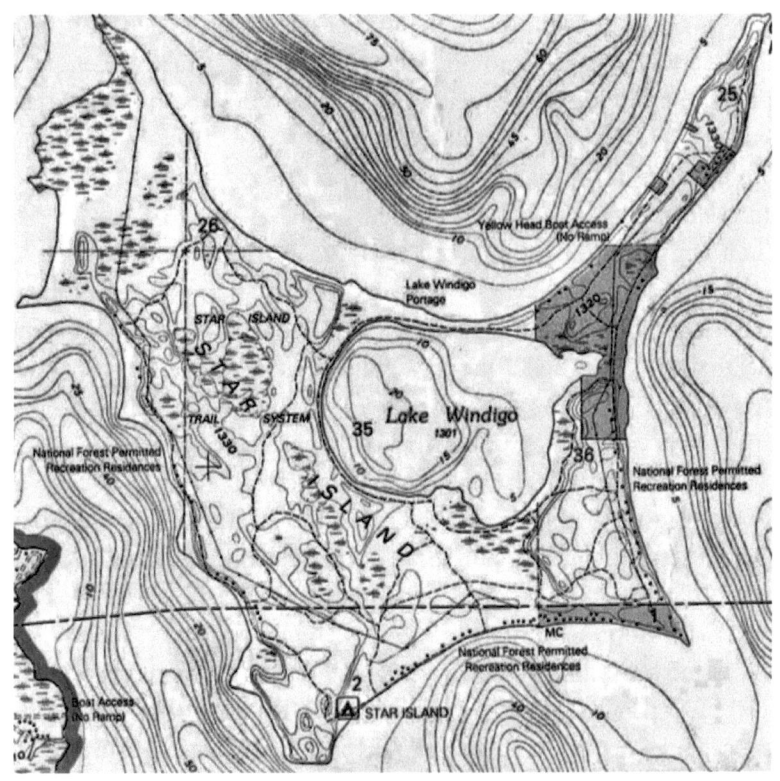

Map of Lake Windigo and Star Island
Image courtesy of USDA Forest Service

7
HATCHETS, TALLOW, AND ICE: SURVIVING LAKE WINDIGO

In northern Minnesota, inside the boundaries of the Leech Lake Reservation sits the feared and unsettling Lake Windigo. The lake is completely enclosed by a five-pointed star-shaped island aptly called Star Island, which in turn is surrounded by the larger Cass Lake. The oddity of Lake Windigo being a lake inside of another lake was made famous in a Ripley's Believe It or Not cartoon. As you will soon discover, others know of the lake for more dreadful reasons.

Ripley's Believe It or Not! cartoon featuring Lake Windigo

The relatively small lake covers approximately 200 acres and reaches a maximum depth of 25 feet. Encompassing nearly 1,000 acres, Star Island is just large enough to give the lake a tucked away and hidden feel. The lake's name was said to have been derived from the Native people of the area who believed that the cursed body of water was the home of the deadly wendigo. In an article extolling the wondrous beauty of the lake, the *Sedalia Evening Democrat* further explained the Windigo name, writing that it means "the place of the evil spirit."

Much of the history of Lake Windigo has been passed down from one generation to the next in the oral tradition of storytelling, making its true history difficult to piece together as evidenced by the countless differing versions as to why the lake and island are

Our 2015 expedition to the lake
Noah Voss (L), Chad Lewis (M), Kevin Lee Nelson (R)
Photo by Authors

cursed/haunted. Early Native peoples were extremely fearful and apprehensive around the lake, believing that some wicked evil lurked just beneath its waters. Over time, legends began that the lake was the home of the wendigo and many people became convinced that the lake itself was the wendigo.

Wanda McFaggen is a Tribal Historic Preservationist with the St. Croix Chippewa Indians of Wisconsin. As a guest on the TV show *In Search of Monsters*, McFaggen expressed the belief that the wendigo "is a being that came from water, we do water ceremonies to appease the spirits of the water—that's where he came from, maybe that's where he lives." The idea that the monster lives and lurks in the icy water seems to corroborate early tales about visitors going out on the frozen lake only to discover large holes in the ice with gigantic footprints coming from the holes and leading straight to the island. It is as though the wendigo rose up out of the ice and made its way to the island in search of its next prey.

In his wonderful book, *Dangerous Spirits: The Windigo in Myth and History,* Professor Shawn Smallman also explored the water nature of the wendigo. When speaking about indigenous peoples' understanding of one particular wendigo, he wrote, "This Windigo was very unusual in that it existed under the water, and it seemed to be unconnected to cannibalism. It reflected an emerging trend in the mid-twentieth century in which Windigos sometimes became associated with water spirits."

Several children have lost their lives from drowning in the lake; some have placed the blame on deadly quicksand-like mud positioned around the shoreline, while others believed that the hungry wendigo would snatch the children from the shoreline and pull them down to their watery graves. Early warnings about the lake featured countless stories where the wendigo's insatiable hunger for human flesh forced it to use the lake as a giant kettle where it boiled its victims before devouring them, giving rise to the legend that the lake was a wendigo kettle. Parents warned their children that the lake was to be avoided at all costs—especially at night—a fear that continues to this very day!

In times of severe famine, some Cree and Ojibwe tribes would perform a ceremonial wendigo dance or ceremony (wiindigookaanzhimowin). This dance served a multipronged purpose. First, it solidified the seriousness of the cannibalism taboo and reinforced the tribes' view regarding the abhorrent nature of consuming human flesh. The dance also served to combat the wendigo, warding the tribe and thus preventing the wendigo from devouring or possessing their people. The sacred ceremony centered around drumming circles where tribe members adorned in masks would dance backwards to ward off a wendigo attack. Many researchers and scholars believe that the last known wendigo dance in the U.S. was performed on Star Island.

A weetigo dance photographed at the
Sweet Grass Reserve in 1939
Image courtesy of Saskatchewan Archive Board R-A7671

Many believe the lake is the wendigo.
Noah Voss (L), Chad Lewis (M), Kevin Lee Nelson (R)
Photo by Authors

One of the goriest legends of Star Island tells of an early Native hunting party that was camped out on the island. The men had gone into the woods hunting for game while the women stayed back along the shore and tended to the camp. As darkness fell, the men failed to return. On the second evening, the worried women set off to find the men, eventually discovering their husbands' skinned dead bodies hanging from the trees. Apparently, the men had been freshly killed, as smoke and steam were still wafting off of their peeled bodies. The women believed that the wendigo had struck again. They quickly left the island and vowed never to return, as the island was cursed and full of bad medicine. When others heard the gruesome story, they set out for the island to retrieve the deceased, but no bodies were found. To this day, the bodies of those allegedly skinned men have not been recovered.

In 1976, the Minnesota Historical Society conducted a series of oral history interviews with long-time residents of Star Island in order to capture and preserve their memories of the early days of people permanently living on the island. As you can imagine, tales of these legends varied almost as much as those who were telling them. When asked about the legend of the lake, one long-time resident replied "Windigo was a lake with no bottom in the deep area, and in this bottomless hole a spirit came out at night and ate Indians. And for that reason, the Indians stayed off the Island, and when, at least, I was a teenager that was sort of a scary thing and didn't like to go to Windigo after dark."

One of the most common stories the old timers recounted tells of a young Native woman who against the wishes/demands of her tribe fell in love with a white pioneer man. When she was not allowed to pursue her one true love, she was heartbroken, and looking to end her inconsolable sadness, drowned herself in Lake Windigo. More sinister versions of the same tale tell that the young woman had been killed by her own tribe, or by the white pioneers who also disapproved of the forbidden courtship. In yet another version, the man and woman disregarded everyone's objections, followed their hearts, and got married. Shortly after their wedding they were enjoying a leisurely walk along the shore of Lake Windigo when suddenly a giant monster sprang out of the water and grabbed the woman and dragged her to the bottom of the lake. Shortly after her tragic death (whichever version you believe) the woman's vengeful spirit could be seen rising up out of the lake looking to exact revenge on those who had wronged her. For many years, the lake was called Lake Helen—apparently in honor of the murdered newlywed and her restless spirit.

Avoiding the lake should be only one part of your survival plan, as Star Island itself is full of haunted stories as well. In 1989, Stanley Johnson interviewed longtime island caretaker Otis Marsh. As one of the only year-round residents of the island, one of Marsh's main duties was to care for the unoccupied homes and property that dotted the shoreline during the winter when the island was completely abandoned. Marsh's interview was turned into a small book titled *The Haunts of Star Island*. In the interview Marsh recounted many of the unexplained events that took place on the island.

- Marsh had constant trouble with the windows at one of the homes. Every couple of days he would find that the home's windows were wide open, forcing him to head home, fetch his key, go inside, and close the window. A few days later a window would once again be inexplicably wide open. These were the crank type windows that the wind simply could not open. It happened so frequently that eventually Marsh resorted to nailing the windows shut—which solved the problem.
- Oftentimes lights in some of the cabins would be mysteriously turned on, yet when he checked it out, no one could be found in any of the homes. He would then shut off the lights only to find them on again the next night.
- A mysterious smoke would frequently rise out of the chimney of one of the homes, even though no one was occupying it. It happened quite often, yet each time Marsh checked, the fireplace was empty.
- An odd fire-looking light would appear and dance around the island before quickly disappearing into the night. At first, the odd light was deemed to be ball lighting, but it appeared so frequently that that

explanation was quickly ruled out. This will-o'-the-wisp type light was also seen by several additional witnesses on the island.

One of the most notorious of the island legends tells of the vanishing lost cabins on the northwest section of the island. Apparently old plat maps show that seven cabins were once located on this part of the island, yet their purpose and who actually occupied them still remains a mystery, as does any physical evidence of the cabins themselves. Some speculate that it must have been an early logging camp; others claim that while they were hiking around the island they actually stumbled across evidence of a cabin's old foundation, but when they returned to show others of their discovery, the foundation that had been spotted was simply no longer there.

In the winter of 2015, Kevin and I set off for a camping expedition of Star Island and Lake Windigo. We were joined by fellow Back Roads Lore researcher Noah Voss. Even though we had purposely only packed the essential gear necessary to survive the trip, our packs were bursting with food and warm clothing. We even loaded up an additional pull sled to help tackle the heavier camping gear. As perhaps a foreshadowing of our trials to come, when we spoke with several employees at the visitor center in order to determine which route to the island would be the best, they all expressed disbelief that we would be so foolish as to camp on the island in winter. Several even jokingly commented that we might not return alive—at least we all assumed they were joking. As we started our hike across Cass Lake, the frozen snow and endless ice drifts wreaked havoc on the sled, forcing us to continually stop our trek in order to right the tipped over sled. The gusting winds seemed determined to flip our sled over every five minutes, prompting the earlier warnings from the visitor center staff to echo in our heads as it seemed as though the island did not want us to visit.

Hauling our gear by sled to Star Island
Photo by Authors

After several hours of tiresome battling against the brutal elements, we finally made it to the island and began scouring the land for the perfect spot to set up our base camp. Our first piece of business was to gather wood and get a fire started. Not only did we need the fire for warmth and light, but we also had to keep our tallow hot. Tallow is an animal fat—it is also one of the traditional methods of killing a wendigo. It is believed that if you can pour hot tallow down the wendigo's throat, it will melt its icy heart and the wendigo will die. Just exactly how you are supposed to force the tallow down the wendigo's throat is not specified, but nonetheless, we had hot tallow around the fire for our entire expedition and by the time we had properly explored the lake and surrounding island, darkness was fast approaching. With a blazing fire going, Noah and I decided to venture out to the middle of the lake to see if we could conjure up the wendigo, while Kevin remained back at base camp. By now, the icy winds had dropped the temperature to a bone-chilling 30-degrees-below-zero windchill as Noah and I were walking toward the lake. We were also filming the adventure with several cameras attached to our packs. About halfway to the lake Noah stopped to say that our boots were making such a loud noise crashing into the snow that no one would be able to hear what we were talking about. As we paused there for a brief moment, we were startled by something in the darkness as it quickly and loudly scattered into the thick bush. It sounded like something flapping its wings. Eventually we chalked it up to being some large bird of prey or owl (As you read in chapter 3 owls play a significant role in the wendigo legend) making a hasty exit upon our noisy approach; and even though we had not seen anything, it did get our adrenaline going for the rest of the night. Even though we scoured the woods with our lights,

Kevin wanted more of an adventure sleeping in his
hammock in the severe cold.
Photo by Authors

the pitch-black darkness completely concealed whatever had caused the strange disturbance. When we excitedly returned to camp to inform Kevin of our odd encounter, he had an experience of his own to share. Shortly after Noah and I departed base camp, Kevin began hearing the sounds of heavy footsteps moving about as the unknown noise circled the fire. He could hear faint talking or whispering but was unable to decipher any words. Knowing that it was extremely doubtful that anyone else was on the island, he grabbed his axe and searched the perimeter of the base camp for the source of the noises but found nothing.

Later that night, Noah and I had planned to sleep in our tent, but Kevin wanted more of an adventure, so he decided to tempt fate and sleep under the stars in his hammock—remember terrible weather had set in with the wind chill temperature hovering around -30 degrees. When morning arrived, Noah and I got up to check on Kevin's condition and discovered that his hammock was completely covered in snow and ice. We shared a concerned glance with each other, and for a brief moment wondered if Kevin had frozen to death during the long winter night. Luckily, Kevin began stirring inside his sleeping bag. Although he was extremely cold like the rest of us, he apparently was no worse for wear. Noah and I joked about how if he had died, we simply would have left him there on the island as an offering to the wendigo. Yet, in my mind, the fear of freezing to death was no joke, due to a rookie mistake I had made the previous evening. After spending the day breaking trail and exploring all corners of the island, my clothing had accumulated a fair amount of snow and ice buildup, even though I was completely covered in snow gear. During the evening as I sat by the fire, all that clinging snow and ice melted, causing my clothing to take on a heavy dampness. I should have checked all my gear and brushed myself off once I made it back to base camp, but instead I let the excitement of the expedition cloud my judgment and I went to warm up around the fire. It was a stupid decision, and in a few short hours, I would be cursing myself for making it. Later that night, as I was heading to bed, I looked inside our tent and noticed frost and tiny ice crystals clinging to every inch of the tent, giving off the appearance that the tent was constructed out of brilliant diamonds. That is when I noticed the wetness of my clothes and two choices flashed into my mind. I could simply crawl into my bag and suffer as my wet clothes slowly froze into hard sheets of ice (very dan-

Our frozen expedition tent
Photo by Authors

gerous) or I could strip naked and change into some fresh clothes—which were dry but freezing cold. Without hesitation I quickly disrobed as fast as I could and in that short amount of time, the harsh reality of my situation set in. Standing there trying to throw on new thermal gear, I had the terrifying realization that if I didn't get dressed and into my bag in a hurry, I was going to be in a lot of danger. With winds gusting and howling in the -30 degree windchill weather, it didn't take long for the cold to seep deep into my bones. If something went wrong on the island, we had a good 3-hour hike (in daylight) across a dangerous frozen lake in complete darkness just to get back to civilization. That was more than enough time for me to freeze to death or get severe frostbite. Since I was not looking to lose any of my digits on this expedition, I attempted to keep calm by telling myself I could always just wrap myself in my bag and huddle around the campfire until daylight and then go from there. Thankfully, my changing hit no snags and I launched myself into my bag where eventually I would stop shaking and drift into a cold sleep dreaming of the icy wendigo coming for me. Even the most seasoned adventurer learns something from each new expedition and this taste of freezing had once again reminded me of the importance of slowing down and planning out my moves.

The rest of the extremely chilly expedition went on without any ghostly activity or wendigo sightings, and while some may consider the lack of a wendigo appearance a failure, I see it as an overwhelming success. The benefit of getting a short glimpse into how difficult life had been for those dealing with harsh winters was priceless. The endless battle against the elements forced us into the same mindset as of those who had once feared the wendigo more than anything else on earth, (including death), and it ultimately brought us closer to the wendigo legend itself.

After our expedition, I returned to the town of Cass Lake to give a lecture on mysterious creatures of Minnesota for the local middle/high school system. Before I even started my talk, several tribal elders approached me with a request. They told me that they had heard I was going to speak about a certain feared creature that was said to roam the area. Although they dared not even speak the name of the wendigo, I knew exactly what legend they were referring to. The fear of saying the name of a creature or monster stems from the belief that merely mentioning the name of a legend is enough to put you on its radar, and once it knows who and where you are, it will come looking for you. I have found this to be a nearly universal fear as I have encountered this among locals of nearly every country I have visited. Over my two and a half decades of research, I have learned that if you expect various communities to open up and share their long-held stories and legends with you, you need to respect local traditions and beliefs, regardless of whether or not you share those beliefs. Obviously, I told the elders that I would certainly remove the unnamed legend from my program. My words had no more than left my mouth when I saw their body language immediately relax as though some great fear had instantaneously dissipated. At least for the next few hours, we would all be safe from the wendigo.

8
THE OMEN OF DEATH IS COMING: THE WENDIGO OF ROSS, MINNESOTA

Way up in the northernmost woods of Minnesota is the nearly forgotten ghost village of Ross. During the late 1800s, the Township of Ross was known as Indian Village due to the fact that it was mainly inhabited by Native Americans, along with a handful of white pioneer families. One such early pioneer was Jake Nelson. Luckily for us Nelson kept detailed journals of his time in Indian Village, which were published as the manuscript *Forty Years in the Roseau Valley*. Most of the journal is filled with standard history topics, stories of the first settlers, tragic fires, hunting and fishing expeditions, and the like. Yet, hidden among the more mundane happenings of the area are two intriguing entries where Nelson details the area's paranormal legends.

In 1886, Nelson was working on the construction of his family's home when he "noticed a light by a bunch of willows near the muskeg," about a quarter of a mile from Indian Village. Intrigued by the floating light, Nelson asked his friend Billy McGillis if any of the Indians were out camping in the area, thinking that perhaps their campfires might be the cause of the light. McGillis explained that the light was actually caused by some type of gas rising out of the nearby muskeg. According to the local legend, the light would show up in the exact spot each and every year while the Indians unsuccessfully attempted to catch it. Even Nelson tried his hand at seizing the light, writing, "It seemed to float around us and then return to

Indian Village as it looked in the 1800s
Image courtesy of the Roseau County Historical Museum

the same place." Over the years, others also sought to wrangle up the light, but each gave up, claiming that it was too much like "playing tag with the Devil." The mystery of the light has never been fully explained. Skeptics tend to agree with the explanation put forth by McGillis that these lights are nothing more than swamp gas that produce the baffling light show. On the flipside, many contend that these mysterious lights function as though they are controlled by some intelligent force, possibly even by spirits of the dead as the lights often transform in size, shape and color.

Nelson also wrote quite a bit about the life and culture of the Native people living at Indian Village, even detailing some of their superstitions and paranormal beliefs. One such legend told of a creature so bizarre that it stood out to Nelson, who called it the "Ghost of the Indian River." The Natives called it the "Windago." They had

Early pioneer Jake Nelson
Image courtesy of the Roseau County Historical Museum

encountered the creature many times before and believed that the beast was a harbinger of death, as it always seemed to presage the death of someone living in the village. Nelson explained that the creature had been known to the Indians for so long "that they have no traditions of its first appearance." According to Nelson, the first white people to encounter the apparition or creature were Edina Nelson and her brother, Jesse. The siblings were walking to school about a mile west of the village when "they met the apparition in the road." They described the creature as being "eight feet tall dressed in white and having on its forehead, a large bright star." Nelson claims that shortly after the odd sighting, death once again paid a visit to the village.

Even stranger yet is the story Nelson tells of one Mrs. Michinock, who had been ill for several days. She was being cared for by her granddaughter, Anna Mickinock. Anna was in the yard of her grandmother along with Nelson's mother, his sister and Mrs. Warner when Anna stated, "Grandma die pretty soon." She pointed to a "very tall person, dressed in white" walking across the prairie who disappeared from sight near a grove on a small ridge. Sure enough, consistent with the legend, the very next day death took Grandma Mickinock. Her death should not have come as a surprise because in an even more bizarre twist to the story, the villagers claimed that Michinock was over 150 years old. Nelson told of many very old Indians who lived in the village and none of them "knew anything about the childhood days of the old lady."

Although Nelson wrote highly of the Native peoples, he had to believe that the creature was nothing more than Native American superstition—that is, until he spotted the spirit with his own eyes. It came when the young Mickinock family headed off to Canada on a hunting expedition. During the hunt the wife became ill, sat down, and exclaimed that death had taken control of her. Packing up, the family quickly departed Canada and headed back to Indian Village.

Three days after their return, Nelson was in their yard during the afternoon when he saw that "the apparition had risen by the side of the muskeg." Nelson watched the spirit stumble and nearly fall as it passed out of his line of sight. Nelson described the creature as being about "fifteen feet tall, dressed in white lace or some similar material," carrying some type of package in its right hand. By the following morning, the wife was dead.

After seeing the "Windago" with his own eyes, Nelson speculated on the true identity of the spirit, writing, "It is generally supposed that ghosts walk only at night, but all of the appearances of the above mentioned were in broad daylight and in bright sunshine. Whatever it may have been, it was not a hallucination of superstitious fears in the dark."

The Township of Ross is located deep in the Northwoods of Minnesota near the Canadian border, which is fitting due to the abundance of wendigo sightings that have occurred in Canada. Having been on many expeditions in search of the Canadian wendigo, each of which provided a smattering of firsthand stories, I was excited to once again pursue the creature. In 2004, with a long drive ahead of me, I set off for Ross hoping to get closer to the truth of what type of being was roaming the countryside. As the hours passed, I struggled to put an overall picture of this creature together...too many pieces still remained unknown. While Nelson's journal is indispensable to this case, it offers no definitive answers and at times is even confusing with all the varying descriptions of the spirit/apparition/ghost/wendago. On one occasion the thing is reported to be over 8 feet tall, yet when it is spotted again, it is thought to be 15 feet tall. The only consistent aspect of the beast was that it always seemed to be adorned in white. The white lace or material worn by the beast is an interesting feature and bears resemblance to the traditional sightings of a white skinned/furred wendigo. The bright glowing star-shaped object that decorated the forehead of the

The approximate site of Indian Village as it looks today
Photo by authors

creature also seems to be an outlier, driving it closer to the general appearance of a spirit or apparition rather than a flesh and blood animal. From the journals alone it is hard to distinguish the physical makeup of the being. I decided that the only way to discover the truth behind the legend was to explore the land of Indian Village (Ross). With any luck, my digging around the township might just reveal some additional legends of the wendigo.

Pulling into the tiny township of 450 residents, I half expected them to chuckle as they flippantly declared that the wendigo is nothing more than a Native American superstition from a time long since passed. On the contrary, I found that not only did the locals not scoff at the idea, they were actually willing to share some of the most re-cent sightings. I spoke with a couple of local historians who, over the last twenty years, have kept unofficial records of upwards of ten different witnesses that encountered the wendigo while traveling the back roads of Ross. Unlike the sightings of the past, all of which shared several similarities, each of the more recent accounts differed greatly from one sighting to the next. In the modern sightings, the appearance of the creature spanned the entire spectrum…from those who believed that it was a flesh and blood living creature to those who claimed that they could see right through the being and believed it to be more of a supernatural or spiritual entity. The gender of the creature was another sticking point; the wendigo appeared in the form of a female to some, while others swore that it was a male. And, unlike all of the previous encounters, which were exclusively daytime sightings, several of the recent cases occurred during the wee hours of the night. Based on all the reports, the one commonality was that the wendigo was thought to be a biped, as all of the witnesses spotted it standing upright and walking on its two legs as do humans.

Interestingly, the historians mentioned that a couple of the witnesses talked about a bright light that accompanied the creature. For me the inclusion of the light detail adds to the credibility of the sightings, as the only place that this is mentioned is in the obscure journal of Jake Nelson, which is not a bestselling manuscript. Of course, the mentioning of the light could be simply coincidental or tailored on bigfoot accounts where mysterious lights have appeared in the vicinity of the creature.

In studying the paranormal/folklore, I am always fascinated by the morphing and/or progression that a legend goes through. As the years roll by, oftentimes the legend will transform itself into something else. Sometimes the change is subtle like a changing of the date or name, while other legends are altered so drastically, they take on a complete life of their own. In this case, the harbinger of death aspect has all but been dropped from the legend. The historians assured me that, although multiple recent sightings have been reported, they were not aware of any known deaths attributed to the sightings.

In 2013, I received an email from Donald Kakaygeesick. I was familiar with the Kakaygeesick family as Noah, Kevin, and I had just returned from Canada where we had interviewed Robert Kakay-

Chad Lewis(L) with Donald Kakaygeesick (R)
Photo by authors

geesick (Donald's older brother) about a wendigo creature that was lurking around his family home. Donald had heard of our interest in the legend surrounding the Ross area and wanted to talk about a weird encounter that he had in the same general area. Over the next couple years, as this wendigo book got put in the back burner for more time sensitive projects, I stayed in contact with Donald but never had the opportunity to pursue his story in any meaningful way. Then in 2019, I was finally able to meet up with Donald in the Roseau area to record his story.

During the 1970s Donald was a teenager growing up in Warroad (just east of Ross). One summer, when he was around 12 or 13 years old, Donald was out playing baseball with a couple of his cousins and several other kids from the neighborhood. One of the batters smacked the ball into the woods that jutted up to the field around the local community center. Donald ran out to the woods to retrieve the ball, and as he bent down to pick it up, he was astonished to see two large grayish-white feet standing in front of him. He quickly rose up and found himself staring directly at some unknown giant white creature. Without any hesitation Donald frantically darted back off to the presumed safety of his friends, screaming about some wild monster in the woods. Seizing on the courage that comes from being in a large group, the kids formed a posse and zoomed after the creature. Once inside the woods, the kids heard something big running, so they gave chase just as the creature crossed over a road. Now that the thing was out in the open, they were able to garner a better look at the beast's physical appearance. Whatever it was, it was big—at least 10-feet tall. It had pale white skin with some sort of dirty-whitish hair covering its skinny, lanky body. The most puzzling aspect was that in the middle of its forehead it had a bright star shaped light that was glowing. Even though the thing was much faster than the teens, they were able to keep it in sight because it kept tripping and falling as though it was having trouble running. To Donald, it appeared like someone trying to master the art of running on stilts, as the beast continually stumbled and fell. Remember, Jake Nelson also spotted the creature stumbling and falling some 100 plus years ago. This appears to be a physical rarity that only plagues the Ross creature, as we have not located any other cases that mention the creature's unsteady gait. Eventually the creature was able to put some distance between itself and the pursuers by escaping deeper into the woods. Although it could still be heard thrashing through the brush, it was no longer in sight. No one had any idea of what they had just encountered. Donald informed me that at that age he had no knowledge of the wendigo legend. Intriguingly, I found similarities between this creature's forehead light and the mysterious ball of light that had previously plagued the old Indian Village. Perhaps the separate lights were somehow connected—remember, several other witnesses had spotted a weird light accompanying the wendigo creature of the area.

In 2013, nearly 12 years after my initial visit, Kevin and I headed back to Ross to conduct more research. We were once again joined on this adventure by fellow Back Roads Lore researcher, Noah Voss.

Along the way we made a scheduled pit stop in Bowstring, Minnesota in order to visit a place called Riley's Cannibal Junction. Although Cannibal Junction doesn't sound like an appealing name for a bar and restaurant, Riley's is a popular hangout for locals. Inside, the place is decorated in the typical Northwoods Minnesota fashion; taxidermy animals (including a fur bearing fish), cabin décor, and plenty of wood everywhere. Being such an odd place, it only seems fitting that the restaurant has taken on a haunted reputation as many staff and visitors have reported seeing an odd woman floating throughout the building. She seems to be a bit of a trickster and apparently enjoys moving and tossing items from shelves and tables. However, we weren't there for the ghost stories (those were just an added bonus) we were there to dig deeper into the cannibal legend.

Kevin Lee Nelson outside of Cannibal Junction
Photo by authors

Although the details are vague and specifics are sorely lacking, the local legend tells of some sort of skirmish that took place during the 1800s. One of the warring groups became isolated. With their supplies cut off, they quickly ran out of food and resorted to cannibalism to stave off death. Ever since, the area was called "Cannibal Junction." After interviewing several staff members, it was time to head off in search of the wendigo.

We spent several days scouring the back roads of Ross in search of the creature. We set up motion detectors, night vision cameras, trail cams, and staked out the area with the optimistic expectation of coming face to face with the wendigo. After consulting with several local historians and pouring over a seemingly mile-high stack of maps, we finally pinpointed the exact spot of the Native Indian Village encampment. Unfortunately, the area was currently privately

In search of the wendigo, Kevin Lee Nelson (L),
Noah Voss (M), Chad Lewis (R)
Photo by authors

owned and our multiple attempts to secure permission to walk the land failed. However, not all was lost as due to the layout of the land, a lot of the area can be spotted from the side of the road. It was a surreal feeling being so close to the area that was plagued by the wendigo. Since the area has remained relatively undeveloped, it didn't take a lot of imaginative work to get a feel of what life would have looked like 200 years prior. When I first visited this area, I had no idea that the legend from Jake Nelson's time would ever jump into the modern era.

Even though it is 2020, the legend of the Ross area wendigo seems to be as robust today as it was 120 years ago. Maybe it is not as feared as it once was, but it is certainly as well-known. On our return trip home, we scrutinized and analyzed all that we knew about the case and came to the conclusion that the Ross wendigo remained as mysterious and unexplained to us as it did to Jake Nelson.

9

A BATTLE OF SANITY AND SOUL: WINDIGO PSYCHOSIS AND THE BROADER PSYCHOLOGY SURROUNDING BELIEF IN THE WENDIGO

A young woman sits alone listlessly staring off into the distance. She is lethargic, weary, depressed, appearing as though she is trapped in some dream-like stupor that she cannot awaken from. For some time, she has purposefully isolated herself from the others, refusing to eat anything and rarely speaking to another person. Even more troubling is the fact that when she does talk, she insists that her loved ones have transformed into delicious looking game animals like moose and beaver. Soon, the excruciating pain sets in and she complains that ice is beginning to build up inside of her. At night, she wails, writhes, and screams out that she is going to turn into a wendigo and kill and devour everyone in sight. Her terrifying threats have the entire community spooked; something must be done. But what?

Was this woman gradually being possessed by a wendigo spirit, stricken by some physical disease, or merely in the grips of a serious mental disorder? These are the very questions we are going to grapple with in this chapter.

My educational background is in the field of psychology. As a high school student sitting in psychology class, my interest swayed heavily toward the abnormal side of the field. The more bizarre and unusual the phobia, psychosis, or disorder was, the more intrigued I became. I first learned of the theory of Windigo Psychosis as an undergraduate student studying psychology at UW-Stout. From that time forward, I was passionate about discovering what I could about

Mental changes were sometimes accompanied by
unusual physical transformations
Artwork by Johnny Sixgun

the perplexing legend. Eventually, I ended up doing my masters' thesis on students' belief in the paranormal, focusing mainly on how human perception and belief systems affect belief in UFOs, monsters, ghosts, crop circles and many other segments of the supernatural. Little did I know then that my love for psychology would propel me toward a life of adventure searching for the wendigo.

What is Windigo Psychosis?
First step, we have to define what Windigo Psychosis is. Unlike nearly every other mental disorder, Windigo Psychosis is not listed in the Diagnostic and Statistical Manual of Mental Disorders (DSM) which serves as the definitive diagnosing guide for mental health professionals. Instead, many contend that it falls under the category of a Culture-Bound Syndrome—that is, syndromes that are recognized to be contained within one special culture or segment of society.

The American Psychological Association's Dictionary of Psychology defines Windigo Psychosis as, "A severe culture-bound syndrome occurring among northern Algonquin Indians living in Canada and northeastern United States. The syndrome is characterized by delusions of becoming possessed by a flesh-eating monster (the windigo) and is manifested in symptoms including depression, violence, a compulsive desire for human flesh, and sometimes actual cannibalism."

While this is a pretty fair summation of the disorder, it curiously omits the belief in the wendigo among many in the Great Lakes regions of the United States. Furthermore, my contention is that the belief in the witiko (wendigo) was not nearly as isolated as so many previous researchers and scholars have repeatedly asserted. Upon reading many previous academic papers, one garners the perception that the belief in wendigo was confined to a small remote settlement in northwestern Canada, and no place else. This is just simply not accurate. One only needs to consult the immense library of wendigo research to discover the inaccuracy of this belief. In our work alone, we have dug up legends of the wendigo throughout the entirety of Canada, along with numerous locations littered across the northern United States, beliefs and fears that spread and flourished in places that were thousands of miles apart. However, when dealing with a legend as complex and puzzling as the wendigo, some leeway needs to be shown in any attempt to categorize it.

History of Windigo Psychosis

Windigo Psychosis gained prominence in the early 1930s when missionary J.E. Saindon, who worked extensively with the Cree people, began to notice what he called a "sickness" afflicting the peoples who believed in the wendigo. Eerie patterns began forming among people displaying the effects of this sickness. Another original proponent of the theory was Dr. John Cooper, an anthropologist and instructor at Catholic University who coined the term "Witiko Psychosis." In 1933, this theory quickly spread through the aid of many newspapers, including Delaware's *News Journal* which ran an article headlined, "Freak Madness from Hunger Makes Victims Turn Cannibals." The article provides a fascinating insight into the theory, to which Cooper explained, "Victims imagine themselves actually to be the dreaded 'Witiko,' which has a heart of ice and lives on human flesh." Cooper's assessment of the illness seems to align with its current designation as a culture-bound syndrome as he firmly believed "the 'Witiko' madness probably exists in no other part of the world. It is believed and is an example of how the environment of a people can influence their mental ills."

Cooper spent a considerable amount of time with the peoples of Northern Canada and was well-versed in the traditions and beliefs of those living in the wilds. The *El Paso Herald* reported on a fascinating paper Cooper presented at the American Sociological Society where he stated, "about 85 percent of these adult Cree, at least

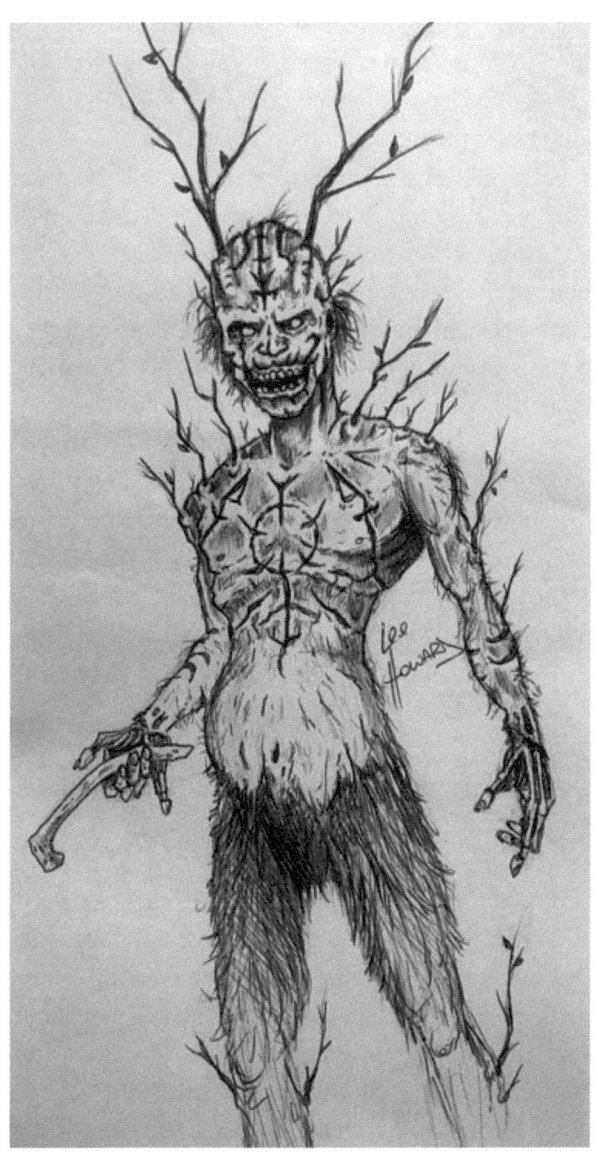

Abrupt changes in personality were often blamed
on wendigo possession
Artwork by Lee Howard

among the women, are subject to hysteria." However, it should be noted that this estimate was based solely on the work of "a priest who has lived for 11 years in their country." Finding firmer footing, Cooper described the most common symptoms of hysteria as "convulsions, hallucinations, melancholia, insensibility to pain, and catalepsy." The overlapping of symptoms between hysteria and Windigo Psychosis is obvious, but Cooper added some stark differences between the disorders, noting that Witiko Psychosis "shows itself as an abnormal craving to eat human flesh and the delusion of being transformed into a Wihtigo," neither of which are necessarily specific components of basic hysteria.

As an early fur trading clerk, George Nelson's thoughts on the topic seem to support the idea that people were suffering from a mental illness as noted in Robert Brightman and Jennifer Brown's book *The Orders of the Dreamed* where they wrote of Nelson's belief that "there is a kind of disease (or distemper rather, and of the mind I am fully persuaded) peculiar to the Crees and Saulteux's, and of which they have the greatest dread and horror."

In 1960, one of the most important and influential works was *Windigo Psychosis: A Study of a Relationship Between Belief and Behavior among the Indians of Northeastern Canada,* by Morton Teicher, who presented his work at the 1960 meeting for the American Ethnological Society. Teicher put together a significant compendium of wendigo legends and stories while claiming "no previous effort has been made to analyze the concept and the illness systematically." Teicher compiled thirty-one wendigo stories from written sources along with seventy people who were thought to have suffered from the psychosis. For his analysis, he focused on the date of occurrence, sex and age distribution of the legends, the number of cases involving cannibalism, and reports of spirit possession. Teicher argued that the relatively small number of wendigo cases was not only dependent on the "fortuitous presence of a white recorder," but "illustrates the way in which a belief may be more important than the facts on which it depends."

For decades, anthropologists, ethnohistorians, and sociologists widely accepted the Windigo Psychosis theory as law. In his wonderful book *At the Font of the Marvelous,* author Anthony Wonderley tells of being taught the theory as an anthropology student in the 1960s. In 1966, the *Winnipeg Free Press* covered the Fourth World Congress on Psychiatry, where Dr. Thomas Boag reiterated the main symptoms as "a compulsive desire to eat human flesh, frequently leading to actual acts of cannibalism, usually directed against family members."

Controversy with Windigo Psychosis

The meteoric rise of interest in wendigo folklore and research was accompanied by substantial shifts in critical thinking as Wonderley noted, writing, "While undergraduates were taking in this sort of thing, their teachers were beginning to wonder about it." By the 1970s, Windigo Psychosis was suddenly the sexy hot topic among research academics, all of whom were looking to add their own updated perspective on the theory, thus creating a wendigo research boom as sparkling new theories abounded. Among the numerous tweaks were many new culprits that could be blamed for the mental illness. In her paper, "A Nutritional Factor in Windigo Psychosis," Vivian Rohrl suggested that nutritional deficiencies could be a factor for the illness, specifically citing the lack of B vitamins (including thiamine) as causing "nervousness, fatigability, changes in disposition, vague digestive disturbances, and anorexia." Rohrl suggested that the use of bear grease (tallow) as a means of curing a wendigo was effective due the high quantities of fat and vitamins contained in the bear tallow—including high concentrations of B vitamins.

Harold Franklin McGee Jr. insightfully questioned the idea of why those suffering from Windigo Psychosis seemed to attack only their own relatives, writing in his research paper, "Windigo Psychosis," "Who else is available? During the period when the windigo is most active people are dispersed in small extended family or nuclear family camps." Utilizing this line of thinking, it makes sense that Swift Runner killed and consumed his own family, as they were the only people around him. Would his choice of victims have remained the same had he been part of a large gathering of people?

By the late 1970s, the entire concept of Windigo Psychosis was being heavily scrutinized. As cracks in the Windigo Psychosis theory began to surface, scholars started questioning whether the entire theory was more symptomatic of those in academia seeking to explain away the perceived hysterical beliefs of a "primitive" culture than data based on an actual belief system among many peoples of Canada. (wendigo beliefs among those in the US were often neglected, ignored, or purposefully omitted.)

In 1982, Lou Marano turned the wendigo research community up-side down with the publication of his paper, "Windigo Psychosis: The Anatomy of an Emic-Etic Confusion." His paper, which he stated was completed after "a review of the voluminous windigo literature enlightened by five years' field research," concluded that "although aspects of the windigo-belief complex may have been components in some individuals psychological disfunction, there probably never were any windigo psychotics in the sense that cannibalism or murder was committed to satisfy an obsessional craving for human flesh." Marano doesn't just contend that the theory inaccurately describes the illness, but that wendigo psychotics never even existed. In fact, when it came to killing a wendigo, Marano expressed the same sentiment as many other researchers, writing, "my major point is that the Northern Algonkians have used the windigo cannibal theme to scapegoat or otherwise divest themselves of the sick, the weak, the marginal, and the disruptive under trying circumstances."

Although I generally disagree with the theory of Windigo Psychosis, my disagreement stems from my belief that tying a mental illness label to people through the lens of hundreds of years, thousands of miles, and a completely dissimilar belief system is ill advised. I also disagree with Marano's latter point that the wendigo belief was nothing more than an excuse for convenience killings. Although I thoroughly explore the fallacy in this line of thinking in the "Curing a Wendigo" chapter, because of its importance, I wanted to additionally point out that many of those who were killed for being a wendigo were young, normally healthy members of the tribe who just fell ill. Not only were they well-liked, they also were hunters and providers for their family units. Killing them would not lessen any hardships faced by the community; in fact, their deaths would often exacerbate the dire predicament that families often found themselves in. Obviously, outliers to this did exist, cases where the person was older, fragile, immobile, or an exorbitant drain on resources, yet these cases were the exception rather than the rule. There is absolutely no doubt that many of the killings were carried out by those who were stricken by overwhelming fear for their own safety and the safety of their loved ones. Accounts of wendigo killings are rife with terror and dread, due to the belief that the infected person would kill and devour everyone in sight, as evidenced by the exorbitant over-the-top measures that were taken to ensure the alleged wendigo was truly dead.

What is puzzling here is that anyone who has read Marano's paper immediately understands that he had obviously conducted deep and extensive research into the legend. The thoroughness of his research makes it even more baffling as to how he could meticulously make his way through the "voluminous windigo literature" and still contend that the killings were done merely out of convenience.

Needless to say, Marano's research (and others) set off a contentious debate that still rages on to this very day. James Waldram touted Marano's work in his book *Revenge of the Windigo,* writing, "Ma-

Were visual and auditory hallucinations responsible
for the wendigo belief?
Artwork by Rick Fisk

rano's (1985) deconstruction of windigo psychosis remains one of the best reminders of the importance of critically reconsidering accepted constructs in the field of Aboriginal mental health." Convinced by Marano's research, Ronald Simons, in his editor role for the book *The Cultural-Bound Syndromes,* takes it a step further, writing, "I, for one, am convinced by the data Marano presents and by the logic of his argument. Thus, I believe that, like members of the Fright Illness Taxon, windigo should no longer be listed among the culture-bound psychiatric syndromes." It should be noted that many scholars found disagreement with Marano's conclusions, including noted wendigo scholar Robert Brightman, who argued that Marano's arguments "seem unduly categorical and the summary explanation of windigo as an 'ideological rationalization' for homicide overlooks evident variation in socio-ecological context and resolution." The debate around Windigo Psychosis will continue to rage on for the foreseeable future. Yet, Windigo Psychosis is not the only proposed explanation as to why people went wendigo.

Were Physical Diseases the Causation of the Wendigo Belief?
Is it possible that the two main psychological symptoms of Windigo Psychosis—the victims' belief that they were physically transforming into a wendigo and the sudden uncontrollable compulsion to consume human flesh were actually brought on by viruses?

Measles, smallpox, influenza, and other infectious diseases ravaged the Native peoples of Canada and the United States—All of these diseases can cause severe delirium in those infected, and many cases of people turning wendigo occurred while the community also happened to be in the deadly grips of a disease outbreak.

The Merriam-Webster Dictionary defines delirium as a "mental disturbance characterized by confused thinking and disrupted attention, usually accompanied by disordered speech and hallucinations." The most common symptoms of delirium read off like a "turning wendigo" checklist—let's take a look:

Hallucinations/Seeing things that are not there–Certainly envisioning your loved ones as tasty game animals would fall into this category, as would seeing a giant cannibalistic monster in the woods.

Calling out, groaning, and making other odd noises–Many victims would spontaneously shout out words, threats, and phrases that would terrify their caretakers, forcing them to take action.

Being quiet and withdrawn–Isolating yourself from others was a tell-tale sign of turning wendigo.

Abrupt personality changes–The notion that the person was no longer themselves may have fed the belief that the wendigo had possessed them.

Apathy, lethargy, and depression–A sudden shift in behavior would have alerted concerned family members, who would have viewed the transformation as a sign of the wendigo's powers.

One would be hard-pressed to ignore the similarities that cross over from the symptoms of delirium and ones displayed by those who were suspected of being a wendigo. Even with all of the noted similarities between the two illnesses we have to be cognizant of the old statistics adage that correlation does not imply causation.

Seasonal Affective Disorder (SAD)

SAD is a type of depression that is brought on by the changing seasons. Typically, symptoms begin in late fall/early winter as the amount of sunlight decreases and subside when the weather improves in spring and summer. Symptoms of SAD include feeling depressed, having low energy, difficulty concentrating, sleep issues, losing interest in activities, feeling sluggish, and social withdrawal, among many others. Notice the similarities of these symptoms to those thought to be associated with turning wendigo. In today's world where modern technology and conveniences have provided us with the most comfortable winters in the history of humankind, it is estimated that upwards of 10 million Americans are greatly affected by SAD, and another 10-20 percent of the population may have a mild form of SAD.

Now imagine living in a time and location where daily life was wrought with significantly more hardships than modern times: extreme winters that were extended by a month on each end, brutally cold weather that was truly inescapable in makeshift lodging, cramped and crowded living spaces, severe isolation, starvation and famine, and no medical facilities to aid in your recovery. Physical diseases and ailments aside, those living in the boreal forests of Canada, along with the coldest part of the U.S., most certainly would have suffered from similar effects as SAD. But would these effects, combined with local legends, beliefs, and customs, have been powerful enough to drive people to insanity and cannibalistic thoughts? Certainly, starvation would have (and has) forced people to resort to survival cannibalism, but what about all the other symptoms of those going wendigo? It is hard to even fathom what the ramifications from living year after year in such brutal conditions would do to a healthy mind, much less a fragile mind that may be more sus-

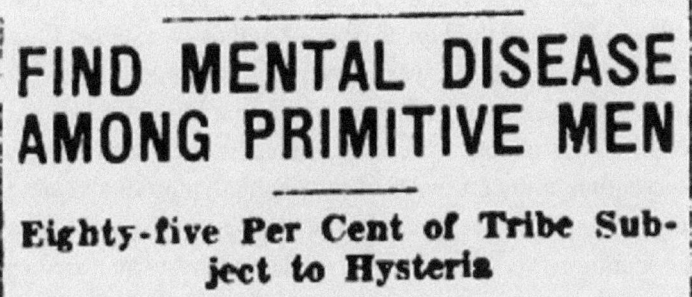

FIND MENTAL DISEASE AMONG PRIMITIVE MEN

Eighty-five Per Cent of Tribe Subject to Hysteria

Newspapers were quick to dismiss belief in the wendigo

ceptible to mental illnesses. I realize that it is impossible to extrapolate today's SAD statistics in order to fit a society existing hundreds of years ago in a much more foreign location where they held completely different belief systems, yet it does provide a general framework to illustrate the general effects of SAD. While SAD is by no stretch of the imagination thought to be the lone cause (or even a major factor) of the mental illness, it seems naive to discount it as simply having no effect.

Suicide by Wendigo?

One of the more fascinating components of those who believed they were turning into a wendigo was their insistent desire to be killed before they fully went wendigo. In today's world, there exists a phenomenon called "suicide by police"—wherein a deranged person who is hell-bent on dying, but for whatever reason is unwilling or unable to commit suicide, forces a standoff with authorities, intent on forcing the police to shoot and kill them. But what if you suffered from the same suicidal thoughts in a culture that was not only devoid of police, but one in which the thought of suicide was linked to weakness?

This theory, which to our knowledge has not been discussed anywhere else, is consistent with suicide by police actions. If someone battling the tremendous forces of mental illness sought to end their lives whether it was to alleviate their suffering or prevent them from killing or harming their loved ones—but they were either too afraid, or for whatever reason were unable to do the deed themselves—they might have seen an opportunity to exploit the wendigo belief to their favor. Instead of forever tarnishing their reputation among the community by committing cannibalism, murder, or suicide, the sufferer could choose to be put out of their misery under the guise of becoming a wendigo. Of course, the request to be killed was not universal among those believed to be turning wendigo; in fact, many victims frantically fought against such extreme measures. Although we can never truly fully understand what was transpiring inside the minds of the victims, the idea of suicide by wendigo makes for an interesting thought experiment.

Oftentimes those who believed they were turning wendigo begged to be killed before the horrifying transformation was complete. Faced with the prospect of becoming a wendigo and suffering an insatiable hunger for human flesh and fearing that they would murder and devour their loved one, many saw death as their only salvation. Let's explore the following case through the lens of suicide by wendigo. In the winter of 1899 at Cat Lake, Ontario, Chief Ah-wah-sa-kah-mig (various other spellings) believed that the wendigo was seeping into his soul. For many days he pleaded with his fellow members to kill him lest he turn wendigo and wipe out the entire tribe. Of course, the tribe was conflicted, one the one hand they were adamantly against killing and losing their beloved chief, yet as chief, his orders had to be followed—not to mention the overwhelming dread and fear that accompanied a person turning wendigo. An article in the *Winnipeg Free Press* noted their dilemma, writing "A council of the tribe was called, and they discussed the matter for two days, when they arrived at the conclusion that the chief's orders would have to be obeyed."

The chief lay down in his wigwam and pointed to the exact spot on his head where he was to be shot. Why he was unable or unwilling to tackle the deed himself is not known. With much dismay, his orders were followed, and he was shot dead. According to the *Hamiota Herald*, immediately after his death "Wood was heaped upon his body and the fire kept going for two full days, thereby, according to the belief of the Indians, thoroughly destroying the evil spirit of their chief."

Word of the killing eventually reached the ears of the authorities who were keen on making an arrest. The only problem was that the people of Cat Lake had not signed any treaty, and therefore were not technically under the supervision of the government. However, special legislation was passed specifically to cover this case and the government sent officers on a 700-mile journey to make the arrests. As was the case with so many other wendigo cases, the tribes people felt they had done nothing wrong and therefore they put up no resistance in returning with the officers. At trial, the men claimed that they had no other options, as the chief of their tribe, his orders had to be followed. Sensing the uniqueness of these circumstances, yet still needing to save face with the general public (who had been feed sensationalized headlines like "Killed A Wendigo," "Killed the Evil Spirit," and "Shot their Chief,") the government eventually got a conviction of manslaughter and gave the men a relatively light sentence of four months in jail. One can easily make the agreement that this case is a prime example of suicide by wendigo. However, this case just as easily demonstrates the intense dread and fear that the wendigo conjured up.

Psychological Fear Spreads Quickly
There is no doubt that general legends about the wendigo produced life-threatening anxiety and colored the perception of everything that was occurring in daily life. Strangers approaching the encampment at night were often met with extreme apprehension. Nightly gales of wind and odd noises were regularly perceived as sure signs of the wendigo's impending arrival. Sometimes hysteria and fear broke out with the mere hint of a wendigo legend. Many of the previous chapters in this book include false alarms and over-reactions to whispers about the wendigo. The overwhelming majority of these tales were never substantiated, nor were they debunked. Yet, once in a great while, actual in-depth investigations were conducted to ascertain the truth behind the chatter.

Sometimes the fear and panic caused by the wendigo took a decidedly deadly turn. In 1897, wendigo fever had reached a boiling point for a young man named Mackekequonabe, living near Rat Portage, (Kenora) Ontario. According to Montreal's *The Gazette*, "The tribe in which Mackekequonabe is a member, have long cherished a superstition that wendigos, or evil spirits, at times appeared in human form." Soon word spread through the tribe that several wendigos were about and "several men were set on guard to watch for them." During one of the night watches one of men left his post "and when his figure was seen in the dark by several of the other guards, they mistook him for a wendigo. They called out to him, but he made no answer, and Mackekequonabe gave chase and shot at him, killing him." Mackekequonabe was put on trial and sentenced him to a six-month sentence.

In 1904 word started spreading throughout northern Minnesota that during the harsh winter near Nett Lake, a man had committed cannibalism. With no game anywhere to be found, the man killed and devoured his wife and child in an effort to avert starvation and thus was susceptible to becoming a deadly wendigo. The *Brainerd Daily Dispatch* reported that "a party was sent to the Indian's cabin at once and will bring him to Nett Lake." News of the cannibal wendigo spread through the entire region, based solely on the word of a man named Gust Brandon, who had been traveling through the area when he heard the gruesome tale. The only problem was that the story was apparently not true. One week after the story of the cannibalism appeared in many newspapers, Indian Bureau officials in Minnesota started an inquiry and sent their Indian Agent, S.W. Campbell, to the area to further investigate. Stephen Gheen, an Indian farmer at Nett Lake, also conducted a review of the evidence. After both investigations were completed, the *Wahpeton Times* reported that the claims "were found to be absolutely without foundation." Even with official word that there was no incident of cannibalism, the damage had been done to the community. Once these legends were put out into the community, they were nearly impossible to contain, regardless of what the truth bore out. This is a prime example of just how fast and far legends of this kind could spread.

In 1912, the *Kalispell Daily Inter Lake* ran an article titled. "Ontario Indians in State of Panic," which told of Indians in the district who were on high alert due to the belief that a wendigo was lurking nearby. While seeing a stranger approach the encampment "They were alarmed at his appearance and ran to cover," abandoning their encampment. The next evening, when the community finally returned, they discovered that the alleged wendigo had made off with their valuables and food.

In 1932, the *Brandon Daily Sun* reported "28 Cree Indians driven from their trapping grounds by superstitious fear of their god Wendigo." Fearing the wendigo, the tribe left their grounds and headed north only to find themselves without any game due to the wendigo's curse. As they slowly marched North in search of game, their health deteriorated and one by one the tribe perished in the unforgiving conditions. The lone survivor relayed the tragic story to the trappers he encountered. One can imagine the countless other unreported cases where the fear of the wendigo was directly (or indirectly) responsible for human death.

The fear of the wendigo isn't merely a historical fear. Terror of the creature has even reached people who have never heard of the wen-

Fear of the wendigo was difficult to contain.

digo. Take one of my recent investigations as an example. In the fall of 2018, as part of the Travel Channel's *In Search of Monsters* episode on the wendigo, I traveled to the Northwoods of Wisconsin to interview Justice and John, two young teenage brothers who believed they both had separate encounters with a wendigo-like creature while away at summer camp. The old rustic summer camp is located a few miles north of the town of Spooner, Wisconsin. Positioned deep in the woods, the camp's sparse buildings and dilapidated looking cabins stick out from the landscape, appearing like a strange lumberjack camp from the 1920s that time had forgotten. The whole area exuded a dark evil creepiness that permeated through the crisp damp air. The entire camp layout looked like some discarded horror movie set. Even though I truly love historical buildings, especially authentically rustic ones, I couldn't believe that any modern-day parent would shuttle their kids off to this camp.

It was just two years prior to our interview that the young brothers found themselves enrolled in the summer camp. Justice, the older

The summer cabin where the creature was spotted

brother, was in his cabin one night enjoying a game of cards with his buddy when suddenly his eyes were attracted to the window by two white lights flickering bright in the night air. At first glance, Justice thought the lights were nothing more than a moth, but as he took a closer look, he noticed that the lights were actually the eyes of some tall odd-looking creature that seemed to be crouched over and peering through the window. Amazingly, Justice locked eyes with the fearsome creature for about five seconds before it swiftly darted out of sight. Desperate to figure out what had been lurking outside his window, Justice told me that "it was definitely something I hadn't seen before, it was humanoid, but it wasn't human." The entire incident left him with the eerie impression that whatever the thing was…it was evil and out hunting for victims! Without knowing the thing's true identity and hoping to avoid raising the fears of his fellow campers, Justice did not immediately report his sighting to any of the camp's counselors.

Although Justice had his sighting through the window of his presumably safe cabin, his younger brother wasn't nearly so lucky. Just one night after Justice had his sighting, John and a friend were wandering towards their cabin (a different cabin) to grab some sweatshirts to ward off the chilly night air. As they got near the lodging John stopped dead in his tracks at the sight of a seven-foot creature standing in the woods. The monster, which John described to me as looking like, "A normal person walking down the street except he had longer legs, longer arms, very tall, and pitch black." John was adamant that the creature wasn't just a person prowling about in the woods—instead, it was something he had certainly never seen before. When John and his friend had first approached, the bone-thin creature appeared to be bracing itself against a tree, but when the twosome walked a bit closer, the thing removed its hand from the tree and became very agitated. Petrified, intimidated, and fearing that the beast was out for blood, John and his friend instinctively started backing away from the monster only to discover that the beast was now moving toward them—so they "ran like no other." John was so shaken by the encounter that he immediately notified the camp counselors so they would be aware that something strange was moving about the camp. A couple of the counselors started a search of the perimeter, not knowing if they would discover a deranged person, a rabid wild animal, or possibly something else. Within a few minutes they caught a fleeting glimpse of something off in the distance, but it quickly ducked deeper into the woods before they could make out what it was. Much to their credit, the counselors took the sightings seriously and immediately implemented a buddy policy—whereby anyone going outside had to have a partner with them.

Location of the second sighting

Upon returning home from camp the two young men started searching online hoping to discover any clues that might help identify the horrible creature they had encountered. Eventually their searches led them to images of the wendigo, a creature they had never heard of before. Immediately they both believed that the creature terrorizing their camp was the wendigo.

While the Northwoods location of the camp and the isolation, along with the fear invoked by the creature certainly meld well with wendigo folklore, several key components of a traditional sightings were missing. First, the encounters occurred in the dead of summer, and while summer wendigo encounters were not unheard of, sightings were much more prevalent in winter. Tie in the fact that there was no hunger, no personality shifts, and no concrete description of the monster(s) and it becomes difficult to ascertain what really happened at the summer camp.

What really intrigued me most about Justice and John's encounters was that even after two years, the fear they had felt was still easily noticeable as they recounted the story—the terror of that time at camp had not dissipated in the least. Additionally, both of the young men struck me as exceptionally honest in the re-telling of their sightings. I gave both of them several opportunities to play up the weirdness of their encounters, but each time the brothers remained steadfast in their original stories. I left the interview with the distinct impression that they were still truly baffled and scared by their time at camp.

Over the last twenty plus years I have received many reports from those who believed they have encountered the wendigo. The locations of the sightings vary widely from Canada to Wisconsin to South Dakota and beyond. These sightings illustrate the continuing belief that the wendigo is not simply a nearly forgotten relic of history.

Conclusions:
When all the on-site research, academic papers, and scholarly books on the subject are boiled down, several questions still remain. 1. Were people actually suffering from a mental disorder that caused cannibalistic beliefs and actions? 2. Is the theory of Windigo Psychosis just another example of "enlightened" people looking to ex-

plain away the beliefs of a "primitive" cultures? 3. Was some supernatural entity actually possessing people?

In answering these questions, I tend to take my cue from H.B.M.
Murphy, a noted figure in the field of transcultural psychiatry who
was concerned by disciplines overlapping where "terms deriving
from one discipline are understood by researchers in the other. Even
within a single discipline terms can be used idiosyncratically, but
the risk of honest misunderstanding is greater when two or more
apply to the same problem." Specifically, Murphy addressed the
limitations of researchers making assumptions and using terminol-
ogy which they did not fully understand. For instance, take one of
the main arguments used to dispute the Windigo Psychosis theory.
Researchers often cite cases in which those who believed they were
turning wendigo were sometimes cured merely by having someone
with perceived power assure them that they would be cured. Skeptics claim that if true forms of psychoses were that easy to cure,
then all the mental hospitals would be empty. Murphy tackled this
very question in his commentary in the book *The Culture-Bound
Syndromes*, writing, "This is a misunderstanding of the term psychosis in its present day and certainly in its transcultural use. Although some psychoses are chronic, many of them, particularly in
developing societies, can exhibit quite rapid improvement."

I feel that it is impractical, or perhaps even disingenuous, for us to
look back on a specific belief which existed several hundred years
ago, within a series of complex cultures and comprehensive belief
systems that are truly alien to us today, and diagnose that problem
not only without ever understanding the cause or prevalence, but
never having even physically assessed someone afflicted by the ail-
ment. It is far too easy to discount the fantastical belief of a supernatural creature inhabiting and corrupting the mind and body of
someone as nothing more than the psychotic ramblings of a crazed
person. Obviously, these people had to be suffering from a serious

mental or physical disorder to believe in the wendigo—but what if they weren't?

What do we make of the accounts from those who dissected alleged wendigo bodies and discovered that the heart was covered in ice, or those who found a line of ice forming on their loved ones' backbone, or in the viscera? Do we simply discount these people as being mistaken, or perhaps suffering from the same mental illness—or were these cases just allegorical tales meant to teach and protect rather than be consumed in a literal form? With no reason to doubt the veracity of those accounts, have we reached the final conclusion based entirely on the fact that the legends are far too odd to actually be true?

We may never truly know the complexities and intricacies that were involved in the belief of the wendigo and wendigo possession. These substantial limitations force us to explain away the wendigo in terms and theories that make sense to how we see the world and our belief systems, even if we do not accurately understand the true nature of the belief.

10
CURING THE WENDIGO CURSE

When the idea is proposed that the wendigo was an actual living being or spirit, many anthropologists, sociologists, skeptics, and various other researchers contend that the legend of the wendigo was simply used by early peoples to help rationalize their approved killing of the mentally ill, the sick, the disabled, the unwanted, while simultaneously lessening the number of mouths to feed during severe famines. In order to absolve them of their guilt, they manifested the belief in the wendigo and wendigo possession. However, I feel this is a gross misunderstanding (perhaps purposefully) of the First Nation, Native peoples, and other cultures. The literature is full of recollections from non-Natives raving of the love and care that Native people expressed for one another. In 1907, the *Manitoba Morning Free Press* shared the very insightful thoughts of an early pioneer, L.R. MacKay, who wrote a letter to the paper claiming, "Of one thing I am certain, the Indians are not guilty of blood-lust in their relationships to members of their own tribe....My experience covering a period of twelve years has led me to infer that the majority of Indians are actuated by more genuine love for friends and relatives than white people are." These sentiments are echoed in one historical account after another, each dispelling the idea that killing an alleged wendigo was done strictly out of convenience to the tribe.

The idea of curing a wendigo makes for an extremely difficult proposition because curing needed to be done before the person fully transformed into the monster. Generally, once someone had gone full wendigo, the only viable remedy was death. Ascertaining the exact point at which someone had fully turned wendigo was extremely subjective.

Here are the most commonly reported cures:

Hot Tallow/ Animal Fat-Grease
Just as tallow was instrumental in killing a wendigo, it was also uti-lized in order to save the life of those turning wendigo. Keeping with the overall complexity of this legend, tallow was thought to work in two completely separate ways. The first tells of the tallow being used to make the victim vomit up the ice growing inside of them or to melt the spreading internal ice. Dr. John Cooper, a re-searcher at Catholic University, who was instrumental in the for-mation of the idea of Windigo Psychosis, told many newspapers in the 1930s that the favorite wendigo curing remedy was "for the vic-tim to swallow hot bear grease, thus melting the heart of ice."

The second purpose of the tallow was to provide lifesaving nour-ishment to those who were starving or refusing to consume anything at all. If we accept the idea that Windigo Psychosis was brought on through starvation and malnourishment, then the consumption of

During our expeditions we are sure to keep our tallow hot over the fire.
Photo by authors

highly caloric substances would certainly aid in the rehabilitation of the victim. The idea of curing a wendigo through nutrition is explored more deeply in the Windigo Psychosis chapter.

Religious Conviction/ Prayer

The influence of belief in higher powers was not limited to Native peoples; the missionaries, pioneers, and fur traders also expressed strongly held dogmas of their own. People of the church often looked upon those turning wendigo as suffering from a mental illness that God could defeat, and lo and behold, it often worked. One such miraculous healing was shared by researcher Colin Thomson who told of an 1850 case where a young woman consumed the flesh of her husband and two children who had died of starvation. Years later, she apparently killed and ate yet another tribeswoman. Eventually, her tribe feared living with her and she was taken to a missionary named Father Arnuad who "put the fear of the 'Great Spirit' into her." The first thing the priest did was to chop off her hair and hang it at the entrance of the Indian cemetery. Then, while kneeling at the church door, she quickly "became converted to Christianity and was cured." This case again illustrates the power of belief and its role in healing of the human mind and body. There are other cases where religious leaders simply told the victims that they were healed. Although detailed records are thoroughly lacking, there are plenty of secondhand stories of religious curing.

Belief in a higher power was frequently used to combat the wendigo

Alcohol

Just as alcohol was implemented in some forms of killing a wendigo, it also factors into curing one as well. George Nelson worked as a clerk for the Hudson's Bay Company in the early 1800s and his writing on the First Nation peoples provides us with a fascinating look inside the wendigo legend and lore from a non-Native perspective. You will discover several mentions of Nelson's critical work throughout our book. Nelson wrote that the only antidote or remedy for curing a wendigo was to "give them large draughts of high-wines; double distilled spirits, or the spirits of wine" that were to be frequently consumed in large quantities while next to a large fire. This was not meant to merely intoxicate the person; the heat and liquor were meant to flow to the heart and thaw the ice that was forming inside the body. Long exposure to heat and heavy sweating also factored into the melting of the ice and subsequent healing of the patient.

Trickery

Wendigo lore is filled with tales of individuals tricking and outwitting the wendigo, sometimes with the aid of a weasel, fox or various other animals. To an outside eye, these whimsical cases certainly would appear more allegorical than factual. However, the Native belief system at the time gave little differentiation between the metaphorical and literal. Similar to how the dream state was equally important as the waking state, the more seemingly imaginative cases were viewed as wholly true. Other cases suggest a more literal and real-world connection to trickery. In *Where the Chill Came From*, Howard Norman included an interesting note about the belief construct between trickery and curing, writing, "One of the old methods of curing spoken by the Swamp Creek elders is to trick an illness into thinking it inhabits the wrong body or that it is not an illness at all." This effect could also be viewed from the perspective of some sort of mental placebo, enabling the victims to simply think away the wendigo and their illness, or believe that it could not harm them. From a psychological viewpoint, this form of mental trickery didn't differ all that much from the religious healings. This belief may also account for the idea that shamans were mostly impervious to the wendigo since they whole-heartedly believed that their shamanic powers would protect them from an evil—including the wendigo. Speaking of shamans…

Powerful Shaman/ Medicine Man

As you have already discovered in Chapter 3, shamans played a crucial role in the societal workings of First Nation/Native peoples. Shamans were both highly revered and tremendously feared due to the power and knowledge they possessed. Shamans were routinely called upon to cure anyone going wendigo. Shamans possessed a wide array of tools and rituals to aid those seeking help and recovery. A shaking tent was frequently used, whereupon the shaman would construct a tent to summon the spirits responsible for the illness (wendigo) and confront them or engage them in battle inside a visibly shaking tent. Powerful animal spirits would also be summoned to help wage a spiritual battle.

One of the more unusual means of shamanic curing came at the hands of Jack Fiddler, Chief of the Sucker Clan, whose amazing wendigo killing days are explored further in the The Last Wendigo Hunter chapter. In their book *Killing the Shamen*, authors Chief Thomas Fiddler and James Stevens tell of a man who was in the process of turning wendigo. Ice had already begun forming inside his body, causing him to crunch loudly as he moved. The man had labored breaths and it was feared he would turn wendigo at any moment. Jack Fiddler was hurriedly summoned and he quickly "picked up two cans and just banged them together and started singing outside this man's tent." Fiddler continued singing as he entered the man's tent—all while staring intently at the motionless man. Without warning "Jack grabbed the man and threw him on the ground. The man got up and Jack threw him down again." The poor man attempted to scream, but only ice flew out of his mouth. Seeing how dangerously close the man was to becoming a wendigo, Jack dragged the man outside the tent and dropped him on the ground. Without hesitation Fiddler took out a whip and began whipping the man. Jack told the turning wendigo, "If you keep doing this thing, I'll whip you to death." Jack continued whipping the man while continually warning him, "If you turn into a windigo, I'm going to kill you, I have the power to do it." After this "healing," the man returned to his normal self and never returned to his wendigo state.

Dog Sacrifice / Dog Lore
This is one of the most obscure means of curing that we have un-earthed, and one where relatively scant information is available. I first stumbled across this method of curing while reading an 1897 newspaper article from the *Edmonton Bulletin* that told of two women who were fleeing their village in terror. Due to their grave illness, it was feared they were turning "witikaw" and thus they needed to be killed. The paper claimed that "The Indians of White Fish Lake were frightened, and they had already sacrificed two dogs to save the two young women, but in vain." Unfortunately, no further details were provided as to why the dogs were sacrificed, the means of sacrifice, or any backstory on the benefits that the sac-rifice would produce. Other researchers have briefly alluded to the fact that in many First Nation narratives, dogs often played the nat-ural enemy to the wendigo, even serving as protection from wendi-gos.

Dogs often were viewed as general protectors from a wendigo, much like they were for other wild animals as well. Several watch-ful dogs could provide an early warning system for any approaching bear, wolves, and yes, the wendigo. Although dogs were excellent at initial detection, this speedy alert didn't always translate into fe-rocious action. Case after case tells of dogs bravely barking loudly before quickly retreating from a wendigo. One such example was chronicled in a 1921 article in the *Winnipeg Free Press* that told of a family that was being visited by a giant wendigo. Each night that the wendigo arrived, "the dogs had been driven growling from the house into the water."

In the 1920 paper, "Native Cemeteries and Forms of Burial East of the Mississippi," David Ives Bushnell reported on the general native custom of sacrifices, writing. "Several sacrifices were also offered; among them were dogs, killed and hung upon the tops of poles .... These, also, were given to the Great Spirit, in humble hope that he would give efficacy to the medicines employed." Although customs differ greatly among various tribes, Bushnell's report does provide a narrow glimpse into the purpose of the dog sacrifices as being meant to assist with the curing of those going wendigo.

Not to get too deep into the weeds on dog sacrifices, but Morris Brizinski and Howard Savage documented several dog sacrifice burial sites in their paper, "Dog Sacrifices among the Algonkian Indians," providing evidence that dog sacrifices were indeed occurring with the First Nation people of Canada, among several others.

Another perhaps tangential connection with dogs and wendigo comes in the belief that dogs, especially black dogs, might actually be a lurking wendigo in disguise. In 1931, the *Hartford Courant* expounded on this theory, writing, "Nobody claims ever to have seen a Witiko but the Indians are in terror when a mysterious black dog prowls about the village. They believe it is one of these monsters in disguise waiting to devour stray children." Of course, this may be a specific belief only to the "Indians" (Atikameks) referenced in the article, yet it would also definitely fall under the larger acceptance among many tribes that the wendigo was indeed a shapeshifter capable of appearing in numerous deadly disguises. Even more contradictory lore comes in the idea that dogs often accompanied the wendigo. Victor Barnouw included several stories of wendigos traveling with dogs in his book, *Wisconsin Chippewa Myths and Tales*, even stating that dogs with the wendigo would engage in battle against dogs from a tribe.

Dogs do present a difficult dichotomy in wendigo lore. On the one hand, as stated above, they could be utilized in the curing and protection from the monster. Yet at the same time, they posed a direct threat of becoming a wendigo themselves. Save for a tremendously powerful shaman, nothing was safe from a wendigo possession—not humans, not animals, not even infants were spared from the wendigo's powers. In 1920, the *Creston Review* published a tantalizingly gruesome account of a dog turning wendigo. In a two-part article, a former Hudson's Bay clerk shared some recollections from his time in the north during the 1870s. These diary-styled offerings spanned everything from humorous mishaps to unique and quirky characters. More importantly, the author recounted the terrible time they had trying to kill a dog that had turned wendigo. After lining up the best dogs in sledding teams, several dogs were left unused, prompting them to become rambunctious and unruly, often stealing other dogs' food during feeding time. One of the especially disruptive canines was a grey husky who "showed the wolf strain plainly and was bad to handle. He had to bite something, either you or his train-mates, so I christened him Wen-di-go." Almost as though it was engaging in a self-fulfilling prophecy, the dog became increasingly aggressive, a trait described by Ruth Landes who wrote "even when a dog is considered windigo (suffering from rabies?) the same phenomena of violence appears."

At one point, the French cook stormed to the leaders proclaiming that "Wen-di-go has turned cannibal." Curious, several of the men dashed out to discover "wen-di-go growling furiously, turning round and round while biting mouthfuls of living flesh out of his haunches and swallowing them, blood, hair and all." Apparently, the bloody, ghastly sight was too much for the Chief who ordered "kill the brute and take him away." The young clerk grabbed a small revolver he was particularly fond of and fired six rounds into the dog's head. After the killing, Wen-di-go's body was dragged down to the ice and the camp was finally rid of the dastardly dog. Well ... not so quick! That very same evening, as all the other dogs gathered around for feeding time, the unconquerable Wen-di-go dog came staggering up the hill "with his head as big as a pail." Its grotesquely swollen bullet-riddled head bobbed back and forth as it meandered toward the food. A council was quickly held, and it was decided that execution was the sentence. This time, they would take no chances and quickly rounded up an axe and block. Wen-di-go's "head was severed from his body and placed on the ice a distance apart." Apparently, decapitation did the trick and Wen-di-go bothered the camp no more. However, those of you astute readers who read the next chapter will clearly see their failure to ensure the wendigo was truly dead.

Obviously, beliefs and traditions have morphed and progressed over the last several hundred years, and during our countless on-site expeditions we have not encountered anyone speaking of modern-day dog sacrifices. Even the mere knowledge of the old rituals has never been broached by anyone we have spoken with. I have no doubt that more literature on dog sacrifices and their relationship to wendigo curing is out there, but as of today, we have discovered little else to give a greater insight into this captivating practice.

11
MELTING HEARTS OF ICE: HOW TO KILL A WENDIGO

As humans, it seems we have an innate desire to protect ourselves from the dangers of non-human beings. It makes complete sense that in order to survive as a species, we would seek to protect ourselves from known deadly animals like bears and wolves, but strangely, we look for protection against mythological or folkloric creatures as well. A shotgun might be well suited to combat the mountain lion prowling around your livestock, but it is unlikely that it would help to ward off the majority of supernatural creatures. History is filled with the superstitions, rituals, prayers, and offerings that are meant to keep the paranormal at bay. Perhaps no other creature elicited the amount of fear that accompanied the wendigo, thereby making it imperative that its weaknesses be exposed.

Over hundreds of years, several means of combating the wendigo have surfaced. Some are practical, some are pretty obscure, but all were trusted to put an end to the dreaded beast.

It should be noted that these methods of killing a wendigo tend to split into the idea of killing the flesh and blood wendigo, while others fight the more spirit-like creature. Some means of death only pertain to those unfortunate victims that had fully transformed into the cannibalistic ice monster. Usually the responsibility of killing a person turning wendigo fell upon the shoulders of a direct family member in order to decrease the chances of retribution coming from committing the act. There is overwhelming evidence that any regular means of death could be used on someone who was merely "going wendigo" or "turning wendigo." At that stage though. the most common ways of killing the future wendigo were through strangulation, an axe to the head, shooting, or stabbing the person to death. Confused? Imagine trying to sort this out when your entire village is scrambling to flee from the arrival of the dreaded monster.

Burn It:

Throughout history, cultures from around the world feared the devastating effects that fire brought with it.. As an undiscriminating force, fire could simultaneously wreak havoc on the townsfolk, and their livestock, buildings, and lodging. Looking for the best way to dispose of the victims of disease and plagues, communities often set them ablaze. Because fire was viewed as such a powerful force, it will come as no surprise to students of folklore to learn that traditionally fire has become a sort of supernatural catchall when it comes to putting an end to paranormal creatures. The idea that fire could bring an end to the wendigo is firmly rooted in the folklore of other beasts. Many innocent victims learned the hard way that one of the best methods to permanently dispose of witches, and thus prevent them from coming back from the dead to seek revenge on those who had wronged them, was to burn their bodies at the stake. In her book, *The Science of Vampires,* Katherine Ramsland, wrote that cremation can also be a highly effective means to dispose of vampires. Cultures throughout the world have also believed that fire was able to destroy the ambiguously defined undead zombie. Again, the overriding theory is that without a proper body to operate from, supernatural beings are unable to thwart death. With so many various supernatural creatures falling victim to fire, it only seems

Noah Voss keeping the fire going—just in case!
Photo by authors

fitting that a creature with a heart made of solid ice would also be bound by the devastating effects of fire. Melting the wendigo's icy heart became the cornerstone of extinguishing its life.

In 1899, a chief in Cat Lake feared he was turning wendigo and ordered two of his tribe members to shoot him before he was fully transformed into the cannibalistic monster. The tribe complied with his orders. The *Logansport Times* detailed what happened next: "After he was dead, wood was heaped upon his body and the fire kept going for two days, thereby, according to the belief of the Indians, thoroughly destroying the evil spirit of the chief."

Noted Cultural Anthropologist Ruth Landes adds further credence to the burning method in her classic book, *The Ojibwa Woman,* by sharing several beliefs of the indigenous people, writing "In the case of the windigos there is additional belief that the ice-skeleton nucleus of a windigo can be destroyed only by burning, that is, by applying fire to melt the ice....Evil shamans and windigos, who are brothers in evil, are cremated instead of buried."

When dealing with a wendigo, it was imperative that all of the body be burned, a point made perfectly clear in *Ojibwe Stories from the Upper Berens River,* where the author noted the belief that if any part of the body was not properly burned, "It will come alive and be stronger."

Fire was also implemented when a suspected wendigo had been killed by normal means. In order to prevent the spirit from simply possessing someone else or coming back alive, the dead body had to be burned and the remains would usually be scattered. The Wisconsin folklorist Charles E. Brown told of one such example in his 1930 monograph *Wigwam Tales,* about an Indian who had fought and killed a wendigo and then "the Indian and his wife gathered wood. They made a big fire and burned the Windigo to ashes."

Hot Tallow:

This method of killing is a bit confusing due to the fact that there is some discrepancy over whether hot tallow will actually kill a wendigo, or if it is merely meant to cure those suffering from wendigo possession (see "Curing the Wendigo Curse"). Regardless of the final outcome, the process of administering the tallow remains the same. The first step is to heat the tallow to the point where it can be directly poured down the throat of a wendigo. Once inside the wendigo, the tallow will thaw the beast's icy heart causing the monster to fall dead.

Hot tallow was used to both cure and kill a wendigo—Today, tallow can easily be found in stores

In his book, *Where the Chill Came From*: *Cree Windigo Tales and Journeys*, Howard Norman included a fantastical story of a wendigo encountering an abandoned village with one young girl surrounded by nothing but kettles full of hot tallow. In an interesting twist on the lore, the girl starts drinking the tallow and with every sip the wendigo cried out in pain before the tallow eventually caused its death.

Out of all the means of killing a wendigo this one seems the most difficult, yet also extremely sensible, since tallow is a form of rendered fat usually taken from a bear or moose or other animal sources, all of which would have been widely available to those living in extremely remote far northern regions of the United States and Canada—at least before severe shortage of game came with the introduction of the fur trade.

Kettles:

Kettles and cauldrons are another recurring motif throughout wendigo lore. They are the only bits of hardware wendigos are said to use or carry with them. Wendigos sometimes use large kettles to cook their victims. In other cases, they use them to carry around human body parts. They may like to keep them close because kettles are also used as weapons against wendigos. In *Dangerous Spirits* Shawn Smallman notes, "In oral narratives, people commonly used kettles to reveal or destroy wendigos." In some wendigo fables the monsters are pushed into kettles and killed. Hot kettles are also used to melt animal fat that is used to melt a wendigo's frozen heart. Additionally, kettles and cauldrons are symbolic for female fertility, the hearth, and abundant food. Smallman continues, "Perhaps because windigos sometimes represented the collapse of the family and social structure (because of predation on relatives), female fertility in oral narratives symbolized a threat to windigos." Kettles (and cooking) also represents heat and fire, an oppositional elemental force to a creature made of cold and ice.

Beware the kettle
Artwork by Rick Fisk

Silver Bullet / Normal Bullet:

Folklore tells of the ability to stop a wendigo by plunging a silver stake through the chest and thereby shattering its icy heart. Likewise, others believed that the monster could be slain only through the use of a silver bullet. Traditionally, the most likely people to encounter the wendigo were the First Nation people. However, the early legends of the wendigo would have certainly been known and influenced by the voyageurs, fur trappers, missionaries, and other early pioneer settlers—many of whom would have brought their own superstitions and fears from Europe. Without a doubt, the later idea of using silver on the wendigo arose by borrowing heavily from the lore of both vampires and werewolves, both of which are said to be susceptible to silver. Many researchers dispel the use of silver and contend that fighting supernatural creatures through the use of a silver bullet is a more modern invention. However, in 1859, a Mr. Paul Kane, who had traveled extensively throughout Canada, wrote into the *Castlemaine Mount Alexander Mail* (an Australian newspaper) that "there is a superstitious belief among Indians that the Weendigo cannot be killed by anything short of a silver bullet." Yet, in the same article, Kane seems to contradict his own statement by recounting a story told to him where an elder woman killed a young female Weendigo by splitting open its head with an ax. Regardless of the apparent contradiction, the article shows that the idea of a silver bullet being used as a supernatural weapon existed much earlier than some skeptics previously thought.

It may be hard to believe that those living a harsh subsistence lifestyle where every winter was a battle just to survive would be carrying around loads of silver, especially silver bullets, yet Ruth

Landes told of the importance of silver among the indigenous people in her classic book, *The Ojibwa Woman*. Landes wrote that "lavish gifts of goods, fur, silver, or horses" were often presented to other tribes as an offering.

Cut Out Its Heart/Cut It To Pieces:
This manner of death also relies on the theory that if a wendigo does not have a body to operate, it will cease to exist—at least with the flesh and blood version of the monster. Yet instead of using fire to dispose of the beast, the wendigo's body is chopped up into numerous pieces that are then scattered, thereby making it impossible for the beast to re-form and continue its killing ways. Obviously, the farther away the body parts can be buried, the more likely it is that the wendigo will remain dead. When Kevin and I visited the community of Wabasca in Alberta, Canada, an area with a long and rich history of wendigo activity, one young woman told us the version of the tale she had heard, that the wendigo terrorizing the town in the old days had been chopped up with pieces of its body buried at the four corners of the town. Often, after a wendigo was killed and buried, large piles of logs would be stacked above its grave as a precautionary measure.

In 1921, an article in the *Winnipeg Free Press* provided more insight into the use of cutting out the heart to extinguish the wendigo. While referencing a crazed man who was "turning windigo," the paper wrote "Tribal custom ruled that he be killed and his heart removed and burnt. Not until this was done could the tribe consider themselves safe from the evil spirit who otherwise would visit them in the isolation of their hunting grounds and devour whole families."

In his book, *Swift Runner*, researcher Colin Thomson wrote of a case where a suspected wendigo was struck with a club before being finished off with a bullet. Once the wendigo was dead, its "battered head was then cut from the body. The Windigo's head was burned to ashes and the body was thrown down a well."

Kill It In The Spirit Realm:
One of the most difficult ways to kill a wendigo was to fight it in the spirit realm. It was said that only a powerful medicine man or shaman would even dare attempt to battle the wendigo due to the deadly consequences that would befall those who failed. A medicine man would enter into the spirit realm through a shaking tent, with the aid of herbs and medicine, or through conjuring rituals, and call upon spirit animals or ancestors for assistance in the grueling task. A 1947 article in the *Winnipeg Tribune* told of another odd trick used by medicine men—whiskey. The paper told the story of one such medicine man who consumed a great deal of whiskey prior to engaging in spiritual warfare, believing that whiskey "rendered him immune from the wendigo while he shouts his incantations in this battle of wills." Apparently, a few years prior, the same medicine man had fought a wendigo and "consumed four bottles of powerful whiskey and ate portions of the bottles. With magic he transmitted the glass shards into the body of the wendigo."

Another side note on alcohol and the wendigo came from an article in the January 11, 1920 edition *Boston Globe* that stated that the wendigo generally "appears around camps just after a supply of drinks has been brought in." This account initially seemed to be just another dig on how the wendigo was nothing more than the savages' drunken illusion brought on by alcohol, but the short article also mentioned that the wendigo "was probably attracted by the smell." If true, the idea of alcohol being an unintentional wendigo attractant was something we had not previously heard of. Part of the difficulty of researching such an old legend, especially one that was mainly shared through oral re-telling, is that we are basically folklore archaeologists trying to fit scraps and fragments of a legend into a coherent lore. How much of the original folklore surrounding the wendigo has been lost to time? How much of a factor did alcohol play in the general terror of the wendigo? One can only speculate as to how much of the legend has been forever lost to time.

Sometimes the inaction of fighting a wendigo in the spirit realm brought about negative social consequences as well. In *David Thompson's Narrative, 1784-1812*, Thompson retold the case where a father was at fault for not calling upon a medicine man to expel the evil spirit possessing his son's body. The medicine men "who by sweating and his songs to the tambour and rattle might have driven away the evil spirit before it was too late."

Hit It With An Axe:

Not a lot of weapons could match the sheer ferocity of a swinging axe. Therefore, it makes sense that if you wanted to stop something from harming you, or even advancing toward you, the axe made for a perfect choice. The wendigo was susceptible to an axe as well. In 1859, the *Castlemaine Mount Alexander Mail* published the allegorical sounding story of an old woman who tricked two wendigos into slipping on the ice in front of her lodge where she "buried the axe in their brains." In his book *Dangerous Spirits: The Windigo in Myth and History*, Professor Shawn Smallman included dozens of cases where a wendigo was killed by the use of an axe.

The wendigo had to be killed at all costs
Artwork by Jamie Snell

Strangle It to Death:

One of the most often applied means of death for a wendigo came in the form of strangulation. It makes sense that this would be a popular choice because you needed no specialized weapons, you simply could use your hands, a rope, or even the person's own hair—as in the 1897 case where according to the *Newark Daily Advocate* a husband grabbed the hair of his wife, who was suspected of turning into a wendigo, and began choking her with it. He used such tremendous force that the pressure eventually snapped her neck. The *Fort Wayne Journal Gazette* expounded on the importance of using the strangulation method in an article featuring another alleged wendigo woman being killed—writing "choking the sick squaw so that the wendigo spirit might not escape with the passing of the victim's breath, but might forever remain imprisoned in the dead body."

The same *Fort Wayne Journal Gazette* article warned that according to Indian custom, bad things would happen if they had not strangled the wendigo, writing, "Should the person die naturally, the wendigo then escapes to the woods and pursues and frightens away game, and famine follows." Famine, of course, would then bring about starvation, which in turn would invite the wendigo back to the encampment and the deadly cycle would be forever repeated.

Conclusions:

With such a plethora of options available to anyone seeking to dispose of the wendigo, it is not hard to believe that countless people lost their lives due to this legend. While the historical killing of suspected Salem witches and others seems to garner all the media, Hollywood hype, and academic attention about killing creatures, those deaths can't hold a candle to the unbelievable number of people that were killed for being a wendigo. Yes, the idea of a witch being burned at the stake provides the perfect imagery for the easily distracted general public, but it is nowhere near as macabre as someone being strangled, then shot, then cut to pieces, then burned, before finally being buried in multiple locations. Also keep in mind that many of those who killed their own loved ones in order stop them from turning wendigo ended up being tried and convicted for murder according to the white man's law, which saw things a bit differently.

Artwork by Iren Horrors

12

THE MODERN MAN-EATER: THE WENDIGO LEGEND TODAY

Myths and legends of all cultures display a myriad of regional variations and permutations. It is especially noticeable with legends spanning large geographical areas. For example, European vampire legends come in countless forms. The Greek *Vrykolakas* is distinct from the Slavic *Upyr,* or the Romanian *Strigoi*, yet all are essentially vampires. The common theme remains the same; they all return from the dead, stalk the night, and drink the blood of their victims. Similar variations in wendigo legends are found between tribes across North America. Like vampire lore, each has its own take on a similar theme. However, inconsistencies in the legend cannot be explained by geographical differences alone; like many cultural beliefs, they also change over time.

Oral traditions in general are more susceptible to change than written records. Without a recorded and canonical version to refer to for periodic recalibration, oral stories have a natural tendency to drift. Much like the "Telephone Game," where stories are told and retold over time introducing variations—subtle or otherwise—each time they are told. Minor alterations, (whether intentional or unintentional), can help place tales within a current context, add emphasis to certain features of the story, or present a lesson in a whole new light. Add into this mix the further complication of translation. Wendigo stories were translated back and forth between different Algonkian dialects, and later between the French and English. Each retelling adds the possibility of embellishment, or adaptation to fit new conditions, to keep tales relevant to new ears. This is the nature, and even the charm, of oral narratives and orally transmitted folk-

lore. Ironically, the latter modifications and distortions of the original tales (if there ever was a true original version) are often the
very elements that keep it relevant and alive. Oral narratives do not
have to be told exactly the same way—what is important is whether
or not they relay the same message. Though inconsequential details
like names and places may change, the key central themes and
moral instructions often remain the same. In the case of wendigo
legends a few features almost always remain the same: ice/cold,
spirit possession, cannibalism and the taboo of eating human flesh,
metamorphosis, and monstrosity.

The Hybridization of Wendigo and French Werewolf Lore
The arrival of Europeans to North America had a profound and irreversible effect on wendigo legends. With the intermingling of cultures through trade, cohabitation, intermarriage, and folkloric
exchange there was an inevitable creolization of monster lore going
on. If there's one thing that people of all cultures like to do when
seated around a campfire at night, it's telling ghost stories and monster tales. Grim and spooky stories are universally loved. The Hudson's Bay Company and the North West Company hired thousands
of French voyageurs and Scottish emigrants to work the fur trade.
The French brought with them tales of shape-shifting werewolves,
and the Scottish brought over stories of the murderous Sawney
Bean and his dreaded cave-dwelling cannibal clan. Both themes, it
was discovered, had a similar domestic counterpart and the legends
easily entwined themselves into aboriginal lore that was already
here.

Wendigo behavior was recorded as early as the seventeenth century.
The earliest reports come from the *Jesuit Relations*. One report,
documented by Father Le Jeune, comes from an incident near Three
Rivers, Quebec. It occurred during the winter of 1634-1635 when
a man, his wife, and their sister-in-law contemplated killing their
brother who they believed was turning into a wendigo and would

attempt to eat them. They described him as, "half-mad; he does not eat, he has some evil design." In another report, Jesuit fathers Gabriel Druillets (1610-1681) and Claude Dablon (1618-1697) along with four Frenchmen and Indigenous canoeists, were on their way to Hudson Bay to establish missions in the region when they encountered something horrific. At Tadoussac they learned of a strange epidemic sweeping through the region, manifesting in severe convulsions and wild behavior. Even more worrisome, the indigenous members of their party were already showing symptoms:

> What caused us greater concern was the intelligence that met us upon entering the Lake, namely that the men deputed by our Conductor for the purpose of summoning the Nations to the North Sea, and assigning them a rendezvous, where they were to await our coming, had met their death the previous Winter in a very strange manner. Those poor men (according to the report given) were seized by a species of disease, which affects their imagination and causes them a more than canine hunger. This makes them so ravenous for human flesh that they pounce upon women, children, and even upon men, being unable to appease or glut their appetite—ever seeking fresh prey, and the more greedily they eat. This ailment attacked our deputies; and, as death is the sole remedy among those simple people for checking such acts of murder, they were slain in order to stay the course of their madness.

Other accounts come from fur traders, like Duncan Cameron (1764–1848), who began trapping with the North West Company north of Lake Superior in 1786. In his journal he painted a picture of a terrifying reality throughout the region:

There are a few who are cannibals by inclination and go about by themselves hunting for Indians with as much industry as if they were hunting animals. The track of one of these is sufficient to make twenty families decamp with all the speed in their power. They look upon those who go about in this manner as invulnerable, so that attempting any resistance is useless, and instead of destroying them whenever, by their number, they have a chance to do so, they make them presents of clothing and provisions, begging them to spare their lives and allow them and their children to live, and the same time acknowledging their lives to be at his or her mercy, women being also addicted to this horrible manner of living.

Early European missionaries, trappers, and explorers did not know what to make of these strange tales and horrific encounters. Keep in mind that in the New World anything could be possible. So much was still unknown to Europeans that the land could be filled with countless undiscovered and unimaginable monsters. This was truly *terra incognita*. A few of the continent's large carnivores, like the grizzly bear, hadn't even been encountered by Europeans yet, though some were kept up at night after hearing Native tales of monstrous mountain bears that dwarfed the eastern black bear.

Not surprisingly, Europeans viewed wendigo phenomena though a Western lens. Many were already familiar with European tales of shape-shifting warlocks who could turn themselves into man-eating werewolves. Lycanthropy (the ability or power of a human to transform into an animal or animal-like state) served as a conceptual template for understanding and defining wendigo phenomena. In her article, "Werewolves and Windigos: Narratives of Cannibal Monsters in French-Canadian Voyageur Oral Tradition, " historian

Carolyn Podruchny states, "The French-Canadian belief in werewolves provided voyageurs with a framework to understand windigos in French-Canadian terms, and in the narratives about cannibal monsters, the motifs of windigo and werewolf mingled."

By the seventeenth century wendigo and werewolf lore was already woven together in the minds of Europeans. In "The Windigo in the Material World" anthropologist Robert A. Brightman notes, "As early as 1695, one French dictionary of an Algonquian language (Bonaventure Fabvre's Montagnais dictionary) glossed the term for windigo as *loups-garoux* "werewolf." The similarities between these traditions became a point of cultural conjunction for Algonquians and Europeans." Even though the nature, appearance, and origin of the two creatures were substantially different, there were enough commonalities between the two beasts for Europeans and indigenous tribes to find common ground around the campfire. Podruchny states:

> Windigos and werewolves were clearly different social phenomena. Windigos were defined primarily by cannibalistic urges, and werewolves were said to crave animals as much as humans. Werewolves were characterized mainly by physical traits, whereas windigos were characterized more by their behavior ... Unlike werewolves, windigos rarely returned to their original human state. However, stories of werewolves and windigos both contained the themes of transformation, magic, and cannibalism.

With every cross-cultural transmission the wendigo and werewolf legends became increasingly bound together. One clear indicator of folkloric cross-pollination is the introduction of the silver bullet into wendigo stories. As early as 1859 the silver bullet, a well-known remedy for destroying werewolves, was introduced as a method to kill wendigos. Podruchny writes, "Both European and Aboriginal stories were not fixed things: They mutated in ways that were fluid, dynamic, and dependent on cross-cultural interaction and exchange. The entangled motifs of windigos and werewolves are reminiscent of many instances of cross-cultural exchange."

In his 1947 article, "The Windigo," published in *The Beaver,* J.A. Burgesse collected two wendigo stories from the Montagnais (Innu) people of Quebec. He noticed that interpretations of the creature had evolved. Some even stated that it was hard to know what a wendigo was because stories and descriptions differed so much from the flesh-and-blood monsters of the past. One story included a wendigo described as something more like a ghost, while the other story described a wendigo as more like a lake monster or water spirit. Neither story had anything to do with a cannibalistic spirit. It's worth noting that even among some indigenous people the concept had evolved into something new. An interpreter told Burgesse, "Nowadays, he said, it is not always easy to recognize a Windigo, which is a very evil spirit, for it manifests in very different forms. In the olden days, however, it had always been a sort of giant, of a stature exceeding imagination." While its transformative nature remained, it had become something far more ill-defined and nebulous. By the late nineteenth century practically any strange and unknown creature prowling the Northwoods was dubbed a "wendigo." In *Dangerous Spirits*, Shawn Smallman writes, "The myths were becoming fractured. The fragments remained, but the lines blurred between different forms."

 The term "wendigo" (or various spellings) became a catch-all for any Northwoods monster or evil spirit. A good example is an article from July 30, 1897, from *The Moose Jaw Herald Times* titled, "The Whitewood Calf-Killer Was a 'Wendigo.'" It is worth reprinting the article here in its entirety to illustrate the confusion over the term "wendigo," as here it is describing a mysterious, four-legged, canid, beast similar to modern sightings of legendary cryptid animals like the "Waheela," "Shunka Warakin," or the "Adlet,":

> It will be remembered that last year a strange beast which got to be known as 'The Calf-Killer' committed great havoc through the district to the south of Whitewood. It ultimately crossed the track and was killed by one of Mr. Frank Cosgrave's sons. Two pelts of a similar animal are now to be seen at Brandon where they were purchased by the representative of Carruther's wool and hide buyers. The beast has no name and is very scarce. Mr. Carruthers says that he has been in the pelt business for thirty-five years, and only has seen three. Years ago the pelt of one was sent to New York, but the New York people were unable to give it a name. It seems probable that the beast is the survival of a race that is nearly extinct. Its color is hard to describe exactly, but it is brown-ish. The head is round, but the nose pointed; and there are resemblances both to the bear and the timber wolf. An Indian saw the pelts in Brandon and said, "Wendigo," and wendigo is Indian for devil, or something of that kind. Our readers will remember that some time ago at Rat Portage [Kenora, ON today] an Indian was tried for shooting another Indian to death believing him to be a "wendigo." The Indians therefore evidently have some superstitions about this rare and elusive beast. The history of the two pelts at Brandon is rather interesting. A farmer found the two beasts devouring a colt of his they had killed. He went back to the house and got a double barrel shotgun loaded with buck-shot. On

returning to the spot the two "wendigos" made for him, and had he been unarmed would undoubtedly have killed him. However, he pumped lead into the foremost, and killed it. The other stopped to sniff at its companion, and he killed it also. It appears that another Indian name is "buffalo runner," as it had a trick of chasing the buffalo in the old days and killing the buffalo calves. The tendency to kill calves in preference to anything else would appear to be inherited. "Wendigo" or no "wendigo," our farmers don't want to see another of this mysterious and destructive brute around.

Confusion over what a wendigo actually is continues to this day. On July 30, 2008 a gruesome murder involving cannibalism aboard Greyhound bus No. 1170 traveling from Edmonton to Winnipeg led to a number of columnists speculating that it was a case of wendigoism. While passenger Timothy McLean was sleeping he was brutally attacked without warning and stabbed to death by Vince Li, the man sitting next to him. McLean was a complete stranger to Li. Once passengers realized what was going on the bus stopped and horrified passengers immediately fled. Li remained on board while the bus driver and passengers held the door shut preventing his escape. During that time Li mutilated, beheaded, and cannibalized McLean. Garnet Caton, who was sitting in the seat in front of the victim, said "He calmly walks up to the front with the head in his hand and the knife and just calmly stares at us and drops the head right in front of us. There was no rage in him…it was just like he was a robot or something." Crisis negotiators tried to reason with Li as a heavily armed tactical unit stood by. Li was arrested and taken into custody after a four-hour standoff when he tried escaping through a bus window.

Li was charged with second-degree murder. He pleaded not criminally responsible (NCR) because of a mental illness and was committed to Selkirk Mental Health Center after being found not criminally responsible of McLean's death. In a 2012 interview with Li, who had subsequently been diagnosed with schizophrenia, Li said:

> The voice told me that I was the third story of the Bible. That I was like the second coming of Jesus. I was to save people from a space alien attack. ... I was really scared. I remember cutting off his head. I believed he was an alien. The voices told me to kill him. That he would kill me or others. I do not believe this now. It was totally wrong. It was my fault. I sinned. But it was the schizophrenia.

In February 2017, The Manitoba Criminal Code Review Board ordered Li's discharge, saying Li does not pose a significant safety threat. Li feels as confused and horrified over his actions as anyone else. Chris Summerville, chief executive of the Schizophrenia Society of Canada says, "He has been a model citizen. He lives every day with remorse about what he did, and he knows that, and he knows it was atrocious, and he will never forgive himself."

Speculation of wendigoism arose immediately after it was discovered that ten days before the killing Li, who had a part-time job delivering newspapers in Edmonton, delivered copies of the Edmonton Sun containing a two page interview with wendigo researcher Nathan Carlson about his research into wendigo phenomena. Those seeking a logical answer to the terrible incident hypothesized that perhaps the article had influenced Li's actions. The Edmonton Sun ran a headline titled, "Bus Beheading Similar to Windigo Phenomena." Except that it's not. The case has very little in common with documented wendigo cases or traditional oral narratives. Mad and inexplicable acts of cannibalism, or having voices in one's head, alone does not justify claims of wendigo phenomena. In Li's testimony there is no mention of starvation, dreams

Artwork by Sarah Terrell

of ice, freezing from the inside, or seeing victims as tasty animals. Instead, in Li's mind he believed he was saving the world from an alien attack. In fact, we do not have any evidence Li even read the Carlson interview.

My home state of Wisconsin is also the unfortunate home of two notorious cannibals, Jeffrey Dahmer "The Milwaukee Cannibal" and Ed Gein "The Butcher of Plainfield." Even though Wisconsin is wendigo territory, neither of the two's horrific actions is ever considered wendigo phenomena. Wild and erroneous speculation surrounding the McLean murder case was perhaps fueled by a desire to sensationalize the terrible events and furthered by an age-old lack of understanding regarding wendigo history and beliefs.

Wendigo Today

Nearly forty years ago Canadian folklorist John Robert Colombo compiled over three hundred years of wendigo reports, tales, poems, and psychological studies in his amazing book, *Windigo: An Anthology of Fact and Fantastic Fiction*. Colombo puts the entire legend in perspective by presenting oral narratives, research, and creative works from a wide spectrum of voices, including Native people, early explorers, anthropologists, psychologists, and artists. It was an instrumental work, as for the first time a large and diverse body of wendigo documents was compiled together showing the depth and diversity of the tradition. At the time of the book's publication the wendigo was an obscure legend mostly limited to a few northern regions. It continues to be fairly limited today, though knowledge of the legend has grown considerably and is more widespread than ever, as suggested by its ever-increasing appearance in pop-culture.

The legend has definite momentum. In fact, just down the road from where I live there is a new restaurant in Stoughton, Wisconsin called "Wendigo" with a tagline "For all beasts, great and small." It's a stylish place with a farm-to-table menu sporting items like the "Cannibal Burger." We believe the wendigo legend is on the cusp of a well-deserved explosion in popularity. At our presentations, audiences have shown tremendous interest and enthusiasm in the legend unlike any other topic. Besides the simple desire for something exotic and new, we feel people are especially interested in lore with North American roots, not just another transplanted and tired European folk tale. It's also a likely reason why stories of Bigfoot, Mothman, and other domestic beasties, like Thunderbirds and Dog-men, are becoming increasingly popular.

There's a reason why it resonates with people. Wendigo themes and symbolism are just as relevant today as they ever were. Just as in earlier times, today the wendigo legend remains a symbol of the dangers of excess and also a dire reminder of the fragility of our humanity. It appears in literature, film, comic books, and even video games, as a reminder that we are always just one choice, or misfortune, away from losing our sense of self, identity—even our very souls—and becoming beasts. A wendigo has only one mindless desire: to eat. It is a lowly and mindless state that is essentially the death of the Self. Furthermore, one of the unique features that makes us human is language and our ability to reason. A wendigo exists in an animal-like state, and other than its baleful wail, it is usually incapable of anything like speech. The absence of language is key to understanding the existential fear of turning wendigo. Without language and reason, one loses personhood and identity. One essentially becomes an object like other forest creatures; a "thing," not a person. This is why the wendigo appears in so many Native parables as a teaching device to serve as a warning. In *Strange Things—The Malevolent North in Canadian Literature*, Margaret Atwood observes that the wendigo is a cautionary lesson that "Humans themselves are potential monsters. The Wendigo is what you might turn into if you don't watch out."

Atwood examines how the wendigo legend has been adopted in literature and pop culture (particularly modern horror). First, and perhaps the most common, is the portrayal of the wendigo as a malevolent manifestation of the environment, or representative of an area's *genius loci*, or spirit of a place. Atwood explains, "It's your presence in the infested location that triggers the experience." Essentially, if you go into the Northwoods, particularly in the winter, you might be in for a big surprise. In these types of stories, the wendigo is the personification of the cold and inhospitable north by representing danger and the unknown. It is the classic struggle of Man vs. Nature, and the wendigo perfectly encapsulates the relentless and brutal indifference of the latter.

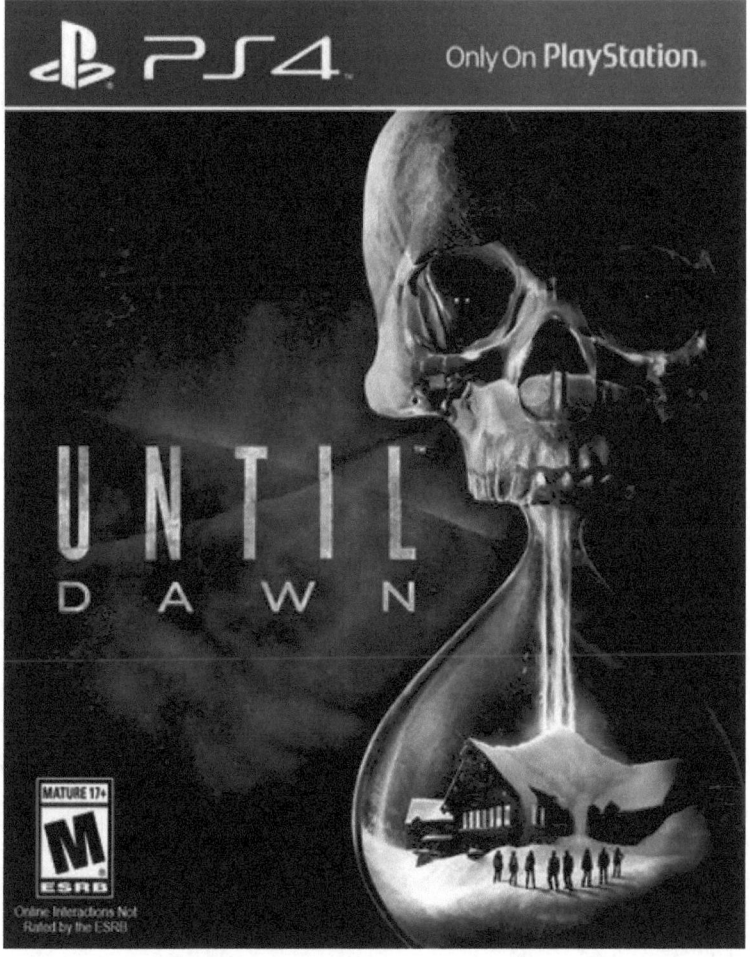

Until Dawn video game
Image courtesy of Supermassive Games

The elemental theme is explored further by Wisconsin author August Derleth in his tales "The Thing That Walked on the Wind" (1933) and its sequel, "Ithaqua" (1941). In both tales the wendigo, which Derleth calls "Ithaqua," is the embodiment of the wilderness and the cold alien vastness of space. But it is Algernon Blackwood's famous tale "The Wendigo" (1910) that inspired Derleth in the first place and best exemplifies the elemental theme of backcountry terror. Set in Rat Portage, Ontario (Kenora today), "The Wendigo" was inspired by tales Blackwood heard while he spent time in the Canadian wilderness. He masterfully invokes a sense of awe and cosmic dread in the reader by the sheer otherness of his creation. His doomed protagonists are at the mercy of something they can barely even comprehend. The tremendous impact of Blackwood's tale on wendigo lore cannot be understated. His tale is largely responsible for creating awareness of the legend outside Native communities and for keeping the topic alive well into the twentieth century, just as stories were starting to vanish among Native speakers.

Blackwood's influence continues over a hundred years later. In 2015, Supermassive Games released a wendigo-themed video game titled *Until Dawn*. Players control the fates of eight young adults stranded during the winter on Blackwood Mountain, an obvious tribute to Algernon Blackwood. In the game the characters are terrorized and hunted down one-by-one by a wendigo, and some even *become* wendigos.

In the winter of 2018, I followed Blackwood's footsteps and traveled to Kenora (the Wendigo Capital of the World). While most of my time in Kenora was taken up by research for this book, I did have time to revisit Blackwood's amazing tale. I hadn't read it since I was a teenager. There was something truly magical about reading "The Wendigo" in the middle of winter at the story's actual location. Fortunately, I didn't meet the same fate as Blackwood's ill-fated protagonists.

Wendigo statue outside Kenora, Ontario
Photo by authors

The wendigo is also used symbolically in pop culture to represent a monstrous fragment of a protagonist's psyche in a Jekyll and Hyde fashion. As Atwoods states, "Fear of the Windigo is twofold: fear of being eaten by one, and fear of becoming one." Sometimes going wendigo is internal, as in a murderous madness or fever of the mind. In other examples it manifests physically through hideous bodily transformation. Both are brilliantly represented in the TV series *Hannibal*, based on the Hannibal Lecter trilogy written by Thomas Harris. In Hannibal, the main protagonist (or even anti-hero?), Hannibal Lecter, enjoys playing games of "Cat and Mouse" with a detective working on murder cases linked to Lecter. Like many serial killers, he lives by a personally subjective code of ethics. For Hannibal, civility, refinement, and common courtesies are the only qualities making humans special and setting us apart from the animals. Therefore, when codes of conduct are breached one forfeits their humanity and is treated as an animal, that is, butchered and eaten. This is further exemplified by one of the show's taglines, "Eat the rude." Throughout the series Hannibal's inner true self is represented as a wendigo (of the modern type with antlers), appearing symbolically through visionary experiences. From the outside Hannibal appears as a polite, if odd, man, but on the inside he is the wendigo and an eater of men.

Mystery novelist William Kent Krueger often uses the wendigo legend in his Cork O'Connor mystery series, set mostly in wendigo country in Northern Minnesota. Krueger approaches the wendigo motif creatively by suggesting that the creature is as much a monster of the heart as it is a monster of legend. It is an evil that can invade people, turn their heart cold, and strip them of their humanity. In *Iron Lake*, Cork's friend Meloux, an old Ojibwe medicine man, warns him, "The Windigo was a man once. His heart was not always ice. What makes a man's heart turn to ice? I would think about that, and I would think about how to fight the Windigo." This is clearly a warning about how the world can make people become hard and cold hearted—even those with good intentions, if they allow it. Later, Meloux tells Cork, "To kill the Windigo, Meloux had said, you must become a Windigo, too. A man was never just a man. A man was endless possibility waiting to become."

In her section, "Consumption, Chaos, and Family Values in The Shining and The Road," included in *The Rural Gothic in American Popular Culture: Backwoods Horror and Terror in the Wilderness* literary scholar Berenice Murphy, brilliantly examines how Jack Torrence, the central character in Stephen King's book *The Shining,* slowly loses his humanity as he takes on wendigo-like characteristics. The Torrence family encounters a situation similar to countless historical wendigo incidents where families find themselves in bleak and desperate snowbound conditions. The references to cannibalism are not subtle. When they arrive at the Overlook Hotel Jack's wife Wendy notes, "The food supplies amaze her, but did not reassure her as much as she might have thought: the Donner Party kept recurring to her." References to the ill-fated Donner Party and their desperate acts of cannibalism pop-up throughout the book (and the film).

As wendigo-like symptoms set in, Jack's physical appearance declines and he starts acting out wildly. In the novel, King describes Jack's metamorphosis by stating that his complexion has changed and that he looks "slightly lunatic." Murphy notes, "He wipes his mouth with a handkerchief so often that his lips begin to bleed. The gesture is a reminder of his alcoholism, but also of his similarity to the Windigo, who in Native American folk art is often depicted as having no lips ... they've been chewed off." In King's novel Jack dies when the hotel's boiler explodes. Death by fire is consistent with how wendigos are traditionally destroyed. Stanley Kubrick's film adaptation of King's novel concludes with Jack getting lost in a hedge-maze and dying from exposure. The film's dramatic final shot of Jack frozen solid is an obvious connection to the "turning-to-ice" belief in wendigo lore. King clearly has an appreciation for the wendigo legend, as the creature appears again as a major antagonist in his novels *The Girl Who Loved Tom Gordon* and *Pet Sematary*.

Viewers of HBO's epic fantasy drama *Game of Thrones*, based on the *A Song of Ice and Fire* fantasy novels by George R. R. Martin, may notice something very familiar about the series' most terrifying villains, the "White Walkers." Martin's creatures are surprisingly similar to wendigos. Martin's White Walkers live in the North and travel with the snow and ice. They are icy corpse-like creatures with freeze-dried flesh that prey upon humans. On the surface they appear almost identical to wendigos. The main difference between

White Walker from HBO's Game of Thrones
Image courtesy of HBO

Martin's frozen undead sorcerers and the wendigo is the White Walkers' eerie patience and composure. Being essentially immortal, time has little meaning to them. They can afford to be patient. As Count Dracula famously says, "My revenge is just begun! I spread it over centuries, and time is on my side." In contrast, wendigos are anything but calm and collected. Wendigos are restless and savage hunters driven by insatiable hunger, whereas White Walkers are sinister tacticians seeking to erase humanity.

It's likely the wendigo will continue to play an evolving role in pop culture. In a culture grown tired of vampire romance novels and endless masked slasher films, the wendigo may appear as a relatively untapped resource in a world always looking for something paradoxically traditional yet fresh. It's a complex and uniquely North American legend that definitely deserves more attention. Fantasy and horror writer Kim Newman perhaps sums it up best when he says, "There is still an ambiguity about what it is: cryptid, evil spirit, shapeshifter, wicked impulse, embodiment of the wilderness, enhanced cannibal, antlered serial killer, bad feeling in the woods, godlike eco-avenger. All readings are valid, but also fluid. Ancient lore, yet relatively fresh material, the Wendigo is liable to stick around in fiction and manifest more often and in more variant forms."

Recently, the wendigo legend has been enthusiastically embraced by the town of Manitowoc, Wisconsin through their annual "Windigo Festival." Interestingly, Manitowoc means "dwelling of the great spirit" in Ojibwe. Windigo Fest is held the first weekend in October each year. It is the area's way of kicking off the Halloween season. Now in its fourth year, the festival draws thousands and includes live music, vendors, food, a costume parade, guest speakers, and an art exhibit. During the festival's very successful inaugural year I interviewed festival organizer Dawn Marie Dabeck, who also runs a horror-themed B&B she calls a "Dead & Breakfast." When I asked her why she chose the wendigo theme for the event Dabeck said she wanted a scary and mysterious theme that was local to the area, or at least the Great Lakes region. Furthermore, she explained that Wendigo is considered one of the great manitous, so it made sense to have Windigo Fest in Manitowoc. Dabeck prefers the "Windigo" spelling because she feels it "sounds like a spooky wind and fits with the season." Just like the wendigo of legend, the festival continues to grow bigger and bigger, expanding each year with new events and larger crowds.

Windigo Fest in Manitowoc, Wisconsin
Photo by authors

Modern Attributes

Cannibals and Consumption—Wendigo as a Symbol of Modern Greed

In his introduction to *Sudden Storm—A Wendigo Reader*, Larry Fessenden, director of the film *Wendigo* (2001), comments, "The Wendigo is different in every portrayal...but at its core, it signifies the evils of rapaciousness and a world out of balance. And while histories and circumstances shift, the essence of the Wendigo persists." Fessenden continues, "Because its origin story is not rooted in Western literature or folktales, Hollywood films or American comics, there are no definitive characteristics to restrict the way it appears or the exact meaning it evokes. It is a Rorschach creature signifying much about our place in the world." Fessenden is correct. Traditional wendigo themes like gluttonous consumption, predatory behavior, and suspicion of outsiders are still relevant in the modern era. They can manifest as xenophobia and fear of strangers, and also through anxieties over scarcity fueled by overconsumption in an ever-shrinking and overburdened world. In *The Manitous: The Supernatural World of the Ojibway,* author Basil Johnston echoes this idea when he states, "New Weendigoes are no different from their forebears. In fact, they are even more omnivorous than their old ancestors. The only difference is that modern Weendigoes wear elegant clothes and comport themselves with an air of cultured and dignified respectability. But still the Weendigoes bring disaster, fueled by the unquenchable greed inherent in human nature." He continues by saying that today wendigos have been "reincarnated as corporations, conglomerates, and multinationals."

The insatiable desire for luxury furs, particularly beaver pelts during the Fur Trade Era, collapsed entire ecosystems and nearly caused the extinction of a number of North American fur-bearing animals. Sustained over-trapping of game animals also contributed to an increase in winter famine among indigenous people who traditionally relied on hunting through the winter to sustain them. Wendigoism and famine are fundamentally linked, so with increased food scarcity came an increase in wendigo reports. Among the Swampy Cree the wendigo has long been a symbol of greed, or something that is out of balance with the environment. In *Where the Chill Came From—Cree Windigo Tales and Journeys,* a Cree elder states, "It is said that sometimes a Windigo appears as a white trapper, often one who poaches food animals with no regard for the environment." In Katherine Pinkerson's novel *Windigo* (1945) a white trapper's greed is the central theme. Aware of the prevalent fear of wendigos among indigenous people, a trapper intentionally sows dangerous panic among tribal communities to remove competition for furs.

Native author Jack Forbes uses the wendigo as a metaphor for Western colonialism, imperialism, and exploitation of other cultures in *Columbus and Other Cannibals*. Forbes calls "Wetiko Disease" a "disease of aggression against other living things and, more precisely, the disease of consuming other creatures' lives and possessions." Forbes notes wendigo-like features are baked into the predatory business models of exploitative companies and the barbarous actions of Western governments. It brings to mind one of lines from the 1999 film *Ravenous,* set in the Sierra Nevadas in 1840 (arguably one of the best wendigo films ever made). At Fort Spencer, Colonel Ives (brilliantly played by Robert Carlyle, a suspected wendigo) succinctly sums up the voracious ethos of a fledgling nation when he says, "This country is seeking to be whole, stretching out its arms, and consuming all it can," implying that through the Westward Expansion the *American Spirit itself* has gone wendigo by growing large and devouring everything in its path. Manifest Destiny has become a merciless and unstoppable *man-eating* destiny.

Paul Levy uses a similar metaphorical comparison in his book *Dispelling Wetiko*. However, whereas Forbes' analogy examines political and economic strategies that emulate wendigo behavior, Levy instead looks at it from a psychological point of view. He uses the wendigo as a metaphor for modern dysfunctions like unbridled consumerism and self-destructive non-sustainable environmental plunder. The wendigo is described as a "parasite of the mind" and a "collective psychosis" manifesting in a fundamental disconnect from the environment and a spiritual emptiness in Western culture. He asserts that in our search for wholeness and connection with the world we mistakenly try to fill the void in our lives with more and more "stuff," and, like the wendigo of legend, we can never be fully satiated. Ever hungry, we continue to seek material wealth as a measure of success and a source of happiness even though it provides no lasting transcendent nourishment, just empty calories. In his article, "The Many Faces of the Wendigo," Chris Hibbard echoes Levy's point when he states, "The Wendigo we have today is much, much worse. It is now purely a metaphor for those things in life that corrupt and lead one astray, such as alcohol, money, gambling, and power."

Levy continues to draw parallels between non-sustainable and destructive environmental policies and wendigo hunger. He comments on how modern society is amazingly oblivious to its own madness and how we are compelled to act against our own (and society's) best interest. This "psychospiritual disease of the soul," as he puts it, manifests as bafflingly short-sighted policy making, like strip-mining in pristine wilderness areas. Land is sacrificed for a few very temporary jobs, leaving a polluted scar on the landscape that is no longer useful, or is even hazardous, to all future generations. Boom/bust cycles inevitably leave communities worse off than when they began with fewer future options. Wilderness areas and local economies are much better served through wise forest management and preservation, as they can generate far more revenue in the long-term via hunting, fishing, and other outdoor recreation indefinitely. This myopic attitude is analogous to the wendigo that eats away its own lips out of hunger. Like an animal, it can only react to immediate needs. There is no foresight, only mindless reaction. Its hunger is temporarily satiated, but at the cost of its own face.

Antlers and Hooves?—How the Wendigo Became a Deer-Man
Many, if not most, contemporary wendigo images depict a creature with the antlers of a stag and occasionally hooves instead of feet. Some artistic variations attempt to represent the concepts of starvation and death by giving the creature what I've come to call the "zombie-stag" look. Typically, renditions of this sort have a pronounced spectral, or undead, look, often with a stag skull for a head and shreds of frozen tissue hanging from the ribs. Clearly the im-

agery is far from the traditional image of the wendigo, so how and where did the modern deer-man interpretation of the legend originate?

It's possible the deer-man image could be various artists' attempts to represent the creature symbolically and is not intended to be a literal representation. It's also reasonable to assume that many artists are not deeply familiar with the actual history behind wendigo tales, especially considering how obscure the legend is. Many assume the wendigo is something like a Northwoods nature spirit, or elemental of the north, though it's hard to blame artists for taking artistic license with the legend considering how difficult it is to find reliable information. Accessing traditional indigenous narratives,

Wendigo Illustration by Matt Fox
for Algernon Blackwood's "The Wendigo" in Famous Fantastic
Mysteries: June, 1944

historical records, and obscure academic anthropological studies can be a daunting task. Without access to authoritative details, artists are inclined to fill in the gaps with their imaginations.

The antler motif likely originated with Matt Fox's incredible wendigo illustration that accompanied a reprint of Algernon Blackwood's tale "The Wendigo" in the June 1944 issue of the pulp magazine *Famous Fantastic Mysteries*. Fox's interpretation of the wendigo shows a gigantic ogre-like creature towering over the treetops with antlers, fur, and eyes blazing like stars. It has a very elemental feel to it and pays homage to the belief that the wendigo is a type of winter spirit. The image also suggests the creature has the ability to control the wind and snow, which it directs with a clawed hand. In its other hand it holds one of the hapless characters from the story as it whisks him away into the wintry night. Fox's vision of the wendigo shows clear Western influence, as it seems to have inspiration from Celtic mythology, specifically a likeness to Cernunnos, the god of the forest and male fertility. He is usually represented with the antlers of a stag. It's clear Fox's (and Blackwood's) interpretation of the wendigo is something more like a boreal demigod, an ancient and inhuman intelligence whose domain is the northern wilderness.

It's also possible that horned or antlered wendigo imagery may have its origins with the *Windigokan,* the so-called "Backwards Medicine Clowns" or "Cannibal Dancers." The Windigokan are a group of ceremonial dancers and healers among the Plains Cree and Plains Ojibwe. Although the group is named after the cannibal spirit, Wendigo, neither cannibalism nor cannibal characters play any part in the group's practices. The leader of the group is one who has been chosen by Pakahk, the Flying Skeleton (more on Pakahk in Chapter 13). Dancers dress in bizarre clown costumes made to look as shabby and ragged as possible. Costumes include frightful masks which they use to frighten away evil spirits. Masks occasionally include long pointed noses and stylized horn-like antlers or pointed ears. It's possible Windigokan masks could be a source for modern wendigo antler imagery, but it is only a theory.

Windigokan dancers use absurd and contrary tactics as part of their healing technique. They do everything backwards: walk backwards; talk backwards—everything is inverted. The dancers are specialists in the removal of bad spirits that cause illness. In "The Plains Indian Clowns, Their Contraries and Related Phenomena," John Plant describes the exorcism process, explaining, "The contrary-shaman would bring his troop of clowns into the lodge of the patient and perform the exorcism rites. With ludicrous movements, the clowns

Traditional Windigokan mask.
Assiniboin Clown wearing leather mask.
Southern Saskatchewan, 1909.
Lowie, Robert H. 1909 The Assiniboine.
Anthropological Papers of
the American Museum of Natural History, 4:1-270

Contemporary wendigo mask from author's collection
Photo by authors

approached the sick, while pounding their rattles, singing, whistling, and dancing. They came up and looked at the patient, became startled and ran away frightened. If the contrary-shaman announced that the sufferer would die, it meant that recovery was certain to occur by the next day."

The deer-man imagery seems to have stuck. In the 2001 film *Wendigo*, directed by Larry Fessenden, a young boy is given a small carved figurine by an older Indian man who says it represents a wendigo. The figurine, or effigy, is a departure from traditional descriptions of wendigos, as it looks more like a stylized anthropomorphic deer-man with a stag's head, human torso, and cloven hooves. Additionally, 2020 will see a new horror film by Scott Cooper titled *Antlers,* based on the short story "The Quiet Boy" by

Nick Antosca. Details about the title's antlered creature have been a closely guarded secret, but many reviewers have suggested that the antlered creature is in fact a wendigo. The wonderfully suspenseful and gory trailer suggests this also.

Hooves have been reported in a few older sightings, so it's not an entirely new development or Hollywood creation. A report of a wendigo in the *Winnipeg Free Press* on April, 8th, 1921, mentions a hoofed creature. Sir Wilfred Thomason Grenfell, a Labrador missionary and founder of Grenfell Mission, records "the visit of an undoubted windigo" at the home of a Scotch settler. The settler measured the tracks in the mud and noted, "The stride was about eight feet, the marks of the cloven hoofs of an ox. The children described the creature as looking like a huge hairy man; and several nights the dogs had been driven growling from the house into the water. Twice the whole family had heard the creature prowling around the cottage and tapping at the doors and windows."

Interestingly, there are other "Deer Man" legends around North America, but most have no connection whatsoever to the wendigo, like the Kewanee Deerman of Kewanee, Illinois. The legend dates to the late 1950s or early 1960s. Deerman is said to have the upper body of a deer and the lower body of a man. It lurks in the area around Johnson Sauk Trail State Park in northeastern Illinois. One thing Deerman *does* share with some wendigo stories is that Deerman is said to be a bad omen. Local lore states that if you see him three times it means you will die. However, themes of cannibalism, winter, ice, and possession are not associated with the Deerman legend. The Kewanee Deerman has more in common with ubiquitous "Lover's Lane" monsters—urban legends popular among teenagers for generations.

In the summer of 2018, we were in Kewanee for Chad's "Bizarre Illinois" presentation at the Kewanee Library. A few older attendees

Home of the Deerman. Johnson Sauk Trail State Park, 2018
Photo by authors

remembered hearing stories of Deerman when they were kids. Afterward, we camped at Johnson Sauk Trail State Park hoping to have an encounter with Deerman. Alas, we must have arrived out of season because Deerman failed to make an appearance. Maybe chronic wasting disease (CWD) got him.

The antler motif has become so entrenched in modern wendigo symbolism that we debated whether or not to have a wendigo with antlers (or a Deerman-like creature) on the cover of this book. Today so many people attribute cervine characteristics to the wendigo that we were a little concerned that readers may not even recognize a traditional wendigo when they see it. We wanted to avoid confusion; however, we also felt it was our job as researchers to portray the beast as historically accurately as possible—even if it's a bit puzzling to some readers. We eventually decided to do an artistic compromise by including a traditional wendigo, but also giving the ghostly suggestion of antlers, using the northern lights in the background.

Wendigo and the Walking Dead

Wendigos are described as looking cadaverous, that is, extremely thin and emaciated with sunken-in eyes, in some cases, even appearing like a swollen and blackened corpse, or a skeleton of ice. In *The Manitous*, Ojibwe scholar Basil Johnson provides a description of a wendigo that is very similar to contemporary portrayals of the undead, "The Weendigo was gaunt to the point of emaciation, its desiccated skin pulled tautly over its bones. With its bones pushing out against its skin, its complexion the ash gray of death, and its eyes pushed back deep into their sockets, the Weendigo looked like a gaunt skeleton recently disinterred from the grave." Considering their hearts are frozen solid they do not have an operational pulmonary system like most living beings; thus, they are not living creatures, at least in a way that we normally define life. Yet they live. The final stage of wendigo metamorphosis implies a would-be-wendigo effectively dies during the transformation process as their heart slows, stops, and freezes over, only to begin a new and cursed stage of un-life, which places them into the realm of the supernatural or the domain of magical and mythical beings.

They are supernaturally strong and resilient (like being unaffected by cold or having regenerative properties) and can only be killed by decapitation or destruction of the heart. If not properly disposed of they will rise from their grave and continue their cannibalistic appetites. One such incident was recorded by William Falconer in the Hudson's Bay Company Archives at Fort Severn in 1774. A Cree man had gone wendigo, threatened to kill his wife, and posed an immediate threat to those around him. Members of his own tribe asked the traders at the fort to execute the man. They refused, although they did tie him up for everyone's safety. He escaped the next day but was captured by his relatives. Not willing to take any further risks, they split his skull with an axe. According to Falconer, the Cree were afraid that after his death, "He would get out of his grave and come back and kill them....Their superstition leads them so far as to imagine people deprived of reason stalk about after death, and prey upon human flesh, such they say are Witik's (i.e., Devils)."

Among some tribes a belief exists that wendigos can only travel in straight lines. This is a common trait attributed to supernatural beings worldwide. In China, ghosts (and especially the Jiangshi—a type of ghost) are thought to only be able to travel in straight lines. It is one of the reasons given for why roads in China are usually curvy. In the British Isles there is a tradition of "Spirit Roads," or "The Old Straight Track." They are straight and sometimes well-worn paths found along the British landscape that the souls of the dead are believed to travel. Authors, like Alfred Watkins, have proposed they follow an invisible energy grid pattern that some attribute to so-called "ley lines." Considering how large and powerful some wendigos are said to be, it makes sense to travel in a straight line if trees and boulders can be easily swept aside. Why go around obstacles when you can just plow right through?

The description and behavior of wendigos is consistent with modern concepts of the "undead," that is, creatures such as vampires, revenants, zombies, and other forms of the "living dead." Generally speaking, the undead are animated corpses, or phantasms with semi-corporeal bodies. Given the description, it's reasonable for readers to interpret the wendigo as just another name for a "Northwoods zombie," but this would be an erroneous simplification ignoring distinctive cultural characteristics closely linked to geography. The lore surrounding the wendigo legend is entirely unique to the Great Lakes region and Canada. It is as different from a traditional zombie (which has its roots in Haitian culture) as a zombie is from a *Draugr* (meaning, "again-walker,") a malevolent, cannibalistic, corpse-like revenant with the ability to curse its victims, in Norse mythology.

The term "undead" can be traced as far back as 1395 (appearing as *vndeedli*) in a John Wycliffe Bible translation. 1 Timothy 1:17 states, "And to the king of worldis, vndeedli and vnvysible God aloone, be onour and glorie in to worldis of worldis. Amen." Traditionally the term broadly meant, "undying," with the word "immortal" being used in later editions, like the King James Bible. It appears in a 1839 edition of Charles Richardson's *A New Dictionary of the English Language* as "Un-Dead" and is defined as, "Not decayed, wasted, destroyed, killed; not mortal." The term could be applied to something like a vampire, but that was not its original context. It was not until 1897 when Bram Stoker used the term "undead" in his classic work, *Dracula*, that the term was given a new and specific meaning. Stoker uses "Un-Dead" to refer specifically to the walking dead, separating them from other supernatural monsters and immortal beings.

> Before we do anything, let me tell you this. It is out of the lore and experience of the ancients and of all those who have studied the powers of the Un-Dead. When they become such, there comes with the change the curse of immortality. They cannot die but must go on age after age adding new victims and multiplying the evils of the world.
> — Bram Stoker, *Dracula*.

Stoker's usage has redefined the term to this day. The current *Oxford English Dictionary* defines it: "undead (in stories) dead, but still able to move, act and (in some cases) think and speak. Vampires and zombies are undead." The concept of the undead is an interesting one because it is deeply tied to the concept of the soul (or lack thereof). Creatures like vampires and zombies are often thought to not have a soul, or if they do, it is a corrupted one. In the case of the latter they are more like mindless machines acting on instinct or dim memory. The original mind and spirit have vacated the body, leaving the corpse to wander independently. Vampires, on the other hand, are a bit more complex. Modern portrayals of vampires typically highlight their wicked cunning and ability to manipulate minds. But unlike zombies, the soul isn't long gone, or in heaven; instead, it is dominated, trapped, and corrupted—essentially damned inside an immortal creature. Only true death (usually by a wooden stake through the heart) can release the imprisoned and tortured soul.

Older vampire legends from Eastern Europe often painted a different picture. In earlier vampire folklore, vampires are described as far more feral. Mind and higher thinking are mostly gone. Like spectral beasts, they roam about in their filthy burial shrouds and prey upon the living. Much like the wendigo, they have supernatural abilities, are driven by ravenous hunger, and often prey upon their own families.

So is the wendigo one of the undead? In his book *The Undead,* Johan Egerkrans seems to indicate; yes, it is, by including the wendigo in his undead bestiary, though he does not provide an argument for why it is included, other than perhaps its grim appearance. It seems the answer is a complicated one, as it would require applying a relatively recent Western concept to a far older tradition, but it is still a conversation worth having for cultural comparison.

Many wendigo tales speak of wendigos returning from the grave if they are not destroyed correctly. Dismemberment and burning of a wendigo seem to indicate a fear that the wendigo spirit will always attempt to return. Therefore, the only remedy is to completely destroy the host body, making it impossible for it to reanimate, and forcing the spirit to move elsewhere. On the surface this seems like a clear link to the definition of "undead." Vampires are dispatched similarly. However, there is a difference in how cultures view the concept of "spirit" and how a state of "living death" is perceived. In Western culture the undead break the boundary of the eternal separation between the living and the dead. This is what makes them so creepy. It is a condition viewed as unholy and a violation of the natural order of existence, as well as the ultimate taboo in Western culture: a violation of the laws of science. In many indigenous cultures those boundaries are not always so explicitly demarcated. From their perspective, the realm of "spirit" is all around us and permeates all things; it is not detached, separated, and reduced to a distinctly binary "celestial vs terrestrial" dichotomy. In the past, they did not see wendigos as a violation of nature per se, as *everything* was nature. Instead, in its advanced state, it was seen as a transgressive and incurable spiritual sickness.

There are many other parallels between wendigo phenomena and the undead. Wendigos are known for being able to increase their size at will. This is also a feature of the Norse draugr. In Scandinavian lore draugrs are described as looking bloated, having blackened or gray skin, and appearing utterly hideous (also a common description of wendigos). Additionally, many undead creatures and wendigos are supernaturally strong and fast. Stories abound of large ogre-like wendigos towering over trees and covering ground quickly with their huge strides. With the exception of the slow and shuffling zombies made famous by George A. Romero's *Night of the Living Dead* (1968), traditionally the undead have been dangerously quick. It's interesting that in *Dracula* a Transylvanian peasant warns the protagonist, Jonathan Harker, about the undead, saying, "For the dead travel fast." In Blackwood's story, "The Wendigo," after being abducted by a giant wendigo, one of the characters (Défago) screams, "Oh! oh! My feet of fire! My burning feet of fire! Oh! oh! This height and fiery speed," indicating the creature that abducted him is moving so fast the friction is burning his feet. The creature is described as, "quick as lightning in its tracks, an' bigger'n anything else in the Bush, an' ain't supposed to be very good to look at—that's all!"

Where the wendigo legend differs from most undead lore is its lack of association with burial sites. According to most legends of the undead, they tend to haunt gloomy sepulchral locations, like grave-yards and catacombs. Vampires are known for residing in crypts and for needing to return to their coffin before sunrise. Likewise, zombies, wights, draugrs, and reanimated mummies are often linked to cemeteries, burial mounds, and tombs. This is not the case with wendigos. In our research we could not find a single case where a wendigo was associated directly with burial grounds other than their own grave site once they were destroyed, a location that was gen-erally feared and avoided later. One would think that graveyards and burial sites would be prime locations for a cannibal to find human flesh and engage in other ghoulish activity. So, while they are often linked spiritually and symbolically to concepts of "death" and "hunger," much like "hungry ghosts" in folklore worldwide, they are not directly linked to places associated with death and bu-rial, as is commonly seen with the undead. Furthermore, we were able to uncover only a single mention of wendigos involving nec-rophagia, or the eating of the dead. The Atikamekw people of Que-bec described a wendigo to the Rev. Joseph E. Guinard in 1930 as "a giant black man who roams the woods feeding on rotten wood, swamp moss, and corpses." This appears to be an exception among wendigo beliefs. While there are cases of wendigos carrying human body parts with them as grisly trail rations, in every case it was from people they had killed. It appears wendigos generally prefer fresh meat.

Wendigo Whisperings—Mimicry in Modern Wendigo Lore
In modern wendigo lore one often hears that wendigos can mimic human speech, presumably to lure people out into the woods to be

eaten. However, mimicry does not appear in traditional wendigo lore, and appears to be an entirely modern invention. Mimicking human voices to lure people away from safety implies conscious deceit and villainous strategy, which is not something usually attributed to wendigos, as they generally behave like a force of nature with a single-minded desire to eat. Other than howling and wailing, typically wendigo speech is only found in wendigo fables, along with talking animals. It's possible that the power of mimicry entered the lore through Algernon Blackwood's tale "The Wendigo" with the following passage:

> Scarcely knowing what he did, presently found himself running wildly to and fro, searching, calling, tripping over roots and boulders, and flinging himself in a frenzy of undirected pursuit after the Caller. Behind the screen of memory and emotion with which experience veils events, he plunged, distracted and half-deranged, picking up false lights like a ship at sea, terror in his eyes and heart and soul. For the Panic of the Wilderness had called to him in that far voice.

In Blackwood's tale the protagonists experience something similar to a siren song or summoning—a "call of the wild," intended to separate them from the world of men, leading them to their eventual abduction and demise. Blackwood writes, "for the Wendigo is simply the Call of the Wild personified, which some natures hear to their own destruction." Historically, victims of wendigo possession may have experienced something similar after a period of feeling spiritually invaded or having alien thoughts and desires originating from elsewhere. Like a form of schizophrenia, the "voices" in their head may offer a similar summoning, manifesting as a desire to escape into the wilderness to live like an animal. It resembles a mad impulse or drive rather than a form of trickery through imitated voices of family and friends. Blackwood describes the voice as, "A sort of windy, crying voice … as of something lonely and untamed, wild and of abominable power . . . ."

Today wendigos appear frequently on television, like supernatural themed series *Charmed* and *Grimm*. The mimicry theme appears in the series *Supernatural* in the episode "Wendigo" (Season 1: Episode 2). The show's two central characters, Sam and Dean Winchester, are hunted by a wendigo in the Colorado wilderness (not exactly traditional wendigo country). The creature calls out to them in a voice that sounds like someone in distress. Fortunately for the two brothers, they know enough about wendigo lore (or at least the modern additions) to not fall for the wendigo's trickery. When the wendigo is finally revealed, its appearance is refreshingly true to traditional descriptions. No antlers to speak of. When the creature is finally destroyed it is killed through traditional means: fire.

In modern urban legends voice mimicry is a frequent supernatural ability attributed to various monsters and madmen of all sorts. Some versions of the Goatman of Pope Lick legend mention it uses mimicry to lure people out onto an extremely dangerous train trestle outside Louisville, Kentucky, one that has claimed the lives of far too many careless legend trippers out looking for the Goatman. There is also the legend of the Bye-Bye Man in Wisconsin, a supernatural albino maniac that can be summoned via an Ouija board. The Bye-Bye Man allegedly mimics the voices of victims' friends to trick them into letting him into their homes. With these in mind, it's not surprising that unsettling tales of mimicry have found their way into contemporary wendigo lore.

13
CANNIBAL COUNTERPARTS: SIMILAR CREATURES OF THE NORTHWOODS

In the folklore and oral narratives of the North there is a menagerie of cannibal cousins, hungry spirits, and magical beasts sharing the same landscape as the wendigo. Many are regional variations of the wendigo theme unique to specific tribes and are reflections of their particular environments and cultural fears. While many closely resemble the wendigo in characteristics and behavior—sometimes different in name only—they are still distinct beings with their own place in the collective lore of the Northwoods and should not be simply lumped into a "wendigo bucket." Their inclusion here is to demonstrate how widespread tales and beliefs of cannibal giants are throughout the North and to better understand how they could potentially be related or serve as indicators of cultural transmission.

In *At the Font of the Marvelous: Exploring Oral Narrative and Mythic Imagery of the Iroquois and Their Neighbors*, anthropologist Anthony Wonderley argues that traditions of cannibal ice giants extend far beyond Algonkian culture when he states, "The 'mythical Windigo' is not limited to Cree/Chippewa/Ojibwa peoples who employ the word windigo, and . . . a similar or cognate cannibal monster is not confined to the Algonquian-speaking world." Furthermore, John Cooper observed as early as 1933 in his paper, "The Cree Witiko Psychosis," that the Chenoo of the Miqmaq was "obviously identical" to the wendigo of the Cree and Ojibwe, showing that the wendigo concept was widely distributed among Algonkian speakers and beyond from Saskatchewan to Labrador. The fact that cannibal ice giant traditions occupy such an incredibly wide territory indicates the belief system could have a long, and perhaps ancient, history.

The concept certainly isn't limited to North America. Cannibal ice giants can be found throughout the myths and sagas of Scandinavia and the folktales of Lapland in northern Finland. It's interesting how completely separated subarctic cultures created legends of cannibalistic giants that roamed the icy wastes: the wendigo of the Algonkian tribes of North America, the *Jötunn* of the Icelandic/Norse sagas of the North Germanic peoples, and the *Stallo* of the nomadic Sámi of Lapland. Folklorist Charles Godfrey Leland (1824–1903) noted, "It may be observed that while the Chenoo [a North American wendigo-like creature] is a giant with a heart of ice as hard as a stone, the giant Hrungnir, of the *Edda*, has a heart of stone. The Chenoo agrees with the Jotuns in many respects." The Jötunn were fierce giants that came in different elemental forms, most of them "frost giants." Like the wendigo, frost giants were terrifying creatures made of ice. Additionally, they had the power of transformation and were dreadful forces of fear and chaos. Again, like the wendigo, they were grotesque in appearance, had claws and fangs, and fed on humans. Similarly, according to Sámi legends, the Stallo were man-eating giants that roamed the wilderness and tundra of Lapland. Like the wendigo, they could be summoned by shamans and sent to destroy their enemies.

Along with the giants, northern cultures on both sides of the Atlantic also have tales of tribes of mischievous little people. This fact was also noted by explorer Johann Georg Kohl in his accounts of living among the Lake Superior Ojibwe. Kohl notes, "Stories are told of these old fabulous windigos . . . . It is curious enough, too, that the Indian fancy, like that of the Scandinavians and other nations, invented and created a dwarf-like race by the side of the cannibal gi-

Various creatures often dwelled in the Northwoods
Artwork by Rick Fisk

ants." Here Kohl mentions a reference to the Memegwesi, believed
to be a tribe of magical little people, often described as hairy-faced
dwarfs who generally dwell inside caves along large bodies of
water.

One wonders if there is an inherent malevolence present within the subarctic landscape that conjures up specific environmental fears which manifest into ravenous icy horrors in the minds of men. It's an example of parallel thinking where, even though cultures are separated by an ocean and thousands of miles, they share remarkably similar ideas, beliefs, and fears. Or, if one is more metaphysically inclined, perhaps it is a case of "morphic resonance" as posited by author and biologist Rupert Sheldrake, where notions of bloodthirsty ice giants could originate from deep ancestral memories of large and dangerous Ice Age predators that once preyed upon our ancestors.

Oddball Hermits, Wild Men, and Sasquatch

Wendigo stories frequently involve reports of interactions with "wild men" or oddball hermits, often feared, avoided, and suspected of being wendigos. According to Howard Norman in his book, *Where the Chill Came From—Cree Windigo Tales and Journeys*, "Wendigos are sometimes referred to as 'He-who-lives-alone,' or *Upayokwitigo*, roughly 'Hermit Windigo.'" As early as the 19th century anthropologists and missionaries had theorized that perhaps stories of wendigos are actually descriptions of encounters with wild men living alone in the wilderness. Years of living in extreme isolation in the forest may have driven some mad, reduced them to a lowly feral state, or forced them to resort to cannibalism.

Among many tribes in wendigo country there is a general fear of strangers, as one never knows if the person could be a wendigo. In *Ojibwe Stories from the Upper Berens River,* A. Irving Hallowell documents stories collected in 1938 and 1940 from Ojibwe storyteller, Adam Bigmouth. In one story Bigmouth speaks on the anxiety over strangers, stating, "Everyone gets uneasy if he does not know who his neighbors are and does not understand what his neighbor is up to, if there are unidentified strangers about, etc. ... Unidentified persons are potential sources of danger—strangers (piwite [presumably he meant, *biiwide,* the Ojibwe word for stranger]) and there is always the possibility of windigo." In some cases of extreme wendigo panic, like the wendigo panic that gripped Wabasca, Alberta in 1896, strangers risked being shot on sight. It would have been a dangerous situation for an unfamiliar hermit or trapper wandering into a village, especially if they looked disheveled and behaved strangely. In the landmark book *Kitchi-Gami—Life Among the Lake Superior Ojibway*, nineteenth century historian and geographer Johann Georg Kohl comments, "There seems not a doubt that these poor people, persecuted and shot as windigos, are, like our witches, very often wretched persons driven to extremities by starvation."

When writing a study of wendigo lore we would be remiss if we did not address some of the many similarities the creatures share with sasquatch lore, as frequently the behavior and physical appearances of the two creatures are remarkably similar. Both share similar habitat, whether it's the vast northern forests or the far reaches of human imagination. In many early accounts, especially in old newspaper articles, it can be difficult to tell if stories suggest bigfoot phenomena or wendigo cases, as the term "Wild Man" was generally used to describe any strange upright hairy humanoid. The term "sasquatch," derived from "sesquac," meaning "Wild Man" or "Hairy Man," in Halkomelem Salish, the language of the indigenous people of British Columbia, wasn't in common usage then. Furthermore, the term "bigfoot" wasn't coined until the late 1950s, so any bizarre hairy beast was simplified to "Wild Man" in reports.

At times, the two legends are so similar that they get intermingled by storytellers. Both describe large, tall, and (sometimes) hairy creatures. Sasquatch (or bigfoot), like the wendigo, is also known for making loud shrieks, or "vocalizations," a term preferred by modern bigfoot hunters. Additionally, there are many stories of man-eating behavior with sasquatch-like creatures that blur the lines between sasquatch and wendigo legends, particularly the Bukwus and Dzu-nukwa tales from the Pacific Northwest. So, it's easy to see how legends of large cannibalistic monsters sharing the same territory can become interwoven together.

The relationship between the two legends was particularly notice-able to us when we interviewed Robert Kakaygeesick Jr., an Ojibwe artist, visionary, and member of the Buffalo Point First Nation in southeastern Manitoba. Our encounter with Robert was a result of a fortuitous chance event. While we were crossing the border into Canada the Canadian border patrol agent asked us about the nature of our visit. We told him we were folklorists writing a book about a regional legend. Not completely satisfied with our answer, he in-quired about which legend in particular. "The Wendigo," we replied. His demeanor immediately softened. It was clear he was familiar with the term and curious about our research. "You need to speak to Robert Kakaygeesick over at Buffalo Point," he said. He was very excited about our project and said Robert would be a great re-source. He was right.

As instructed, we drove out to the Buffalo Point Cultural Centre and spoke with a member of the staff. We were told they could put us in touch with Robert. They did. Not only that, but he invited us over to his home. We spent part of the afternoon speaking with Rob-ert and meeting his delightful family. Years earlier Robert had an encounter with what he believed was a wendigo, as did his brother some years before that (see Chapter 8). When we asked him what it looked like he said it looked like a "white bigfoot." He saw it standing near a tree line. Robert believes that the two creatures are basically one and the same, or at least closely related. He thinks wendigos are spiritual beings and not entirely flesh-and-blood, ex-isting somewhere between our world and the spirit realm. The en-counter made a tremendous impact on him, and now the wendigo/bigfoot is a favorite subject in many of his paintings. His opinion about the wendigo was surprising to us because it did not really fit the traditional definition held by First Nation Ojibwe. Robert is a good example of how legends can take on new interpretations, especially when impacted by direct experience. It also illustrates how Native people do not hold a single monolithic belief, or feel culture-bound to traditional concepts, but instead possess a multitude of differing beliefs and opinions as varied as any group of people.

Other Man-Eating Ice Giants of North America

Baxbaxwalanuksiwe (also Baxbakualanuxsi'wae, Baqbakualanusi'uae, Baqbakua'latle):

Translating as "Cannibal-at-the-North-End-of-the-World," Baxbaxwalanuksiwe is a man-eater from the oral narratives of Kwakwaka'wakw people of British Columbia near Vancouver Island. Its appearance is perhaps one of the most horrific of all the northern cannibal giants, as it is described as a humanoid bear-like giant covered in gaping bloody mouths. The mouths of Baxbaxwalanuksiwe are always snapping and gnashing, and making the call "hap, hap, hap" ("eat, eat, eat").

Bukwas (also Bakwas, Bookwus, Bukwis):

Bukwas is known as the "Wildman of the Woods" and "Chief of the Ghosts." It is another fearsome creature from Kwakwaka'wakw lore. Bukwas has a creepy appearance, often represented as a thin sasquatch-like creature with long stringy hair. However, unlike sasquatch, Bukwas is considered a ghost-like creature. Like the wendigo, it is emaciated and corpse-like. Tribal masks representing Bukwas often accentuate its ghoulish appearance by giving it green skin. Bukwas is often associated with drowning victims and their restless spirits. It often tempts people with ghost food to turn them into spirits like itself. This is similar to how in dreams the wendigo spirit temps victims with human flesh disguised as food. Bukwas is said to live in a house in the forest that is invisible during the day. Bukwas is served by monstrous supernatural birds called *galuk-w'amhl*, meaning "Crooked Beak of Heaven." Their duty is to provide Bukwas with fresh human meat. They have dramatically hooked beaks that symbolize hunger.

Chenoo (also Chenu, Cenu, Jenu, Tsi-noo, Giwakwa, Kee-wakw, Kiwakwa, Kewahqu):

The Chenoo is a variation of the man-eating ice giant legend from the five Wabanaki tribes: Mi'kmaq, Maliseet, Abenaki, Penobscot, and Passamaquoddy. In *The Journal of American Folklore* article "Penobscot Tales and Religious Beliefs" folklorist Frank Speck (1881-1950) states the Chenoo variant word "kiwakwa" means "going about in the woods." They often have impenetrable skin of ice or stone. They can sometimes be very still and disguise themselves as piles of boulders and blend into the surrounding forest. They are in many ways similar to the Stone Coats of the Iroquois. Like the wendigo, many were once human but now have a heart of ice (though with the Chenoo the heart is often shaped in the form of a man, or sometimes a frozen figure can be found inside its body). In some tales, Chenoos have been cured by forcing them to vomit out the human-shaped ice. Also like the wendigo, they chew away their lips out of hunger, and they have a terrifying scream. It can be kept away by drawing crosses on trees. There is also a general belief that after a powerful shaman dies, they can sometimes rise from the grave as a malevolent Chenoo.

Dzunukwa (also Dzoonokwa, D'Sonoqua, Tsonoqua, Cannibal Woman):

Dzunukwa is a cannibal giantess from the traditions of the Kwak-waka'wakw people of British Columbia. She is called "Wild Woman of the Woods" and "Basket Woman." The latter nickname stems from the belief that she carries a large basket on her back for abducting disobedient children to eat later. She is described as a

Wendigo interpretations have changed over the years
Artwork by Rick Fisk

lumbering and somewhat dimwitted ape-like creature with shaggy
black hair. Because of her ape-like appearance, Dzunukwa is often
closely associated with sasquatch. When not hunting children, she
spends most of her time sleeping in the forest and hoarding treasure.
Representations of Dzunukwa usually depict her with sunken eyes

and wide lips formed into an "O" as if howling or hooting. She is said to make the sound "Hu-hu!" to attract children.

Kaamoowachik:

The Kaamoowachik (meaning "cannibal spirit") is a variation of the man-eating ice giant legend from the Métis tribe. Sometimes the word *Kookoush* is used (derived from Whiitigo) as a general term for any kind of Boogeyman.

Mhuwe (also Mehuwe, Maaleew, Malew):

The Mhuwe is a variation of the man-eating ice giant legend from the Delaware Nation tribes, like the Lenape and Munsee. The Mhuwe is virtually identical to the wendigo in description. One tale states that a Mhuwe stalked a group of hunters and threatened to eat them. They tried to kill it but its skin was too tough for their arrows and guns. Finally, they captured it and killed it by impalement. They staked it to the ground with fire-hardened sticks so that it could not rise again.

Stone Coat (also Ge-no'sqwa, Ronongwaca, Otneyarheh, Thunenhyarhen):

The Stone Coat is an Iroquois and Huron variation of the man-eating ice giant legend and very similar to the Chenoo. While Stone Coats are associated with winter and ice, what makes them different from other wendigo-like creatures is their links to rocks and stone. Their bodies are covered with stony scales as hard as rocks making them invulnerable to most weapons. Other tales say they cover themselves in sticky pine pitch and roll in sand and gravel, giving their skin a stone-like appearance. They were created by Flint (Tawiscara), a villainous trickster in Iroquois mythology associated with night, winter, and death. In most tales, Stone Coats are extremely large. Their gigantic size permits them to carry bear carcasses like squirrels hanging from a belt.

Wechuge:

The wechuge is a creature (or phenomenon) in tales from the Beaver (Dunne-zaa) Tribe. A wechuge is a person who allows their animal spirit to become too strong (usually predatory animals). The tribe believes that each person has an animal spirit, or pawagan, linked to them. Normally the pawagan and the human live in harmony—sort of a mutually beneficial relationship. However, if someone allows the pawagan to become too powerful it will take over the person, both physically and spiritually, and they will become a dangerous wechuge. It is believed that a person who becomes a wechuge will take on aspects and traits of their animal spirit, or even become a large monstrous version of that pawagan. The more dangerous the animal, the more dangerous the wechuge.

In many indigenous North American tribes, power is believed to come through experience, so tribal elders are viewed as the most powerful members of the community. Elders are respected for their restraint and self-control. They have power but use it only when prudent and absolutely necessary. If they abuse their power (a gift from the pawagan), they insult and anger their pawagan. Like any animal, they become more dangerous and difficult to control when enraged. Disrespect feeds it with power, and if they give too much power to their pawagan they put themselves at risk of being dominated by it and becoming a wechuge.

A person can also become a wechuge if their pawagan has been abused or offended by others. The enraged spirit becomes so powerful that it dominates the host. In *Divine Hunger: Cannibalism as a Cultural System,* author Peggy Reeves Sanday states, "Their Wechuge monster dominates the individual whose animal-spirit-friend has been improperly treated by another (usually an outsider). The monster first consumes the individual whose animal-spirit-friend has received this treatment and then turns to consuming others."

In his paper "Wechuge and Windigo: A Comparison of Cannibal Belief among Boreal Forest Athapaskans and Algonkians," anthropologist Robin Ridington gives an example of how wechuge metamorphosis was avoided by a wise elder. Ridington describes a situation where an old man named Jumbie was approached by a stranger attempting to take his picture with a flash camera.

> She did not ask permission to take the picture and when the camera was raised some of the younger people in the camp told her not to take the picture. "Old man he don't like that kind." Although Dunne-za do not like to have their pictures taken without having been given the opportunity to give their consent, the issue in this case was more serious. It was the flash that the old man "did not like." The white woman persisted in attempting to take the picture, and Jumbie, seeing that she would not respect his personal space, dove beneath a sleeping robe in the back of the tent. To the white woman this was an act of fear and reinforced her belief that Indians are child-like and superstitious. To every Dunne-za present, however, Jumbie's action demonstrated his power, not weakness and bravery rather than fear. To have been exposed to the flash would have made him "too strong." It would have risked bringing down to earth the power of Giant Eagle whose flashing eyes still penetrate from heaven to earth in time of storm. The power would have compelled the man to become the Person-eating monster and the man would have lost his own will and judgment to that of the all-consuming monster inherent within himself by virtue of his encounter with it during the experience of visionary transformation as a child.

Wechuge phenomena works in a similar way to wendigo syndrome, and both ultimately result in monstrous metamorphosis. A wendigo possesses someone in a weakened state (spiritually or physically). Similarly, a wechuge is created when a person allows their personal power to be damaged or weakened through pride, breaking cultural taboos, insults from outsiders, or giving into the raw power of their pawagan. Once the internal balance of control shifts in favor of the pawagan, which is their source of supernatural power, they, in essence, become their pawagan and prey on others as that animal would. Sanday states, "If the humans do not respect the other-than-human power of their compatriots, the latter are in danger of being dominated by their animal-spirit power and cannibalizing other humans."

Other Supernatural Beings of the North

Bear-walker:
Bear-walkers are shamans or sorcerers with the ability to shape-shift into animals, particularly predatory ones like owls and bears. There are two types of bear-walkers: those who practice evil medicine to inflict harm on others and those who use magic to assist and cure people. The opposition between "white" and "black" magic practitioners is a common feature in many folk-magic traditions worldwide. In many cases the magical techniques are similar; it is how the magic is *used* that determines whether it is dark or light.

The vast majority of bear-walker lore refers to evil sorcerers, as they are the most feared. They are able to turn themselves into supernatural beasts by wearing the skins of animals. Transforming into animals and gaining their powers through wearing their skins is a common technique in many witchcraft traditions. Bear-walkers often appear to their victims as spectral bears breathing ghostly fire. One bear-walker witness, Alec Philemon, states, "It looked like a bear, but every time he breathe you could see a fire gust. My chum fell over in a faint. That feller on the other side, he faint. When the bear walk, all the ground wave, like when you walk on soft mud or moss." In other instances, they appear as an eerie ball of light drifting around at night. Seeing a bear-walker in any form is an extremely bad omen and usually sickness and death will follow.

Being the target of a bear-walker, or receiving the "bearwalk," a type of curse or hex, will result in misfortune, sickness, and eventual death. When one is magically hunted by a bear-walker it is called being "bearwalked." Bear-walkers strike by sneaking up to victims while in a spirit form and using sorcery to make them faint, fall asleep, or become paralyzed. While victims are immobilized the bear-walker attacks them by magically inserting objects inside the victim intended to cause sickness and pain. If not cured, victims will slowly sicken and die. It is believed that on the fourth night after a victim's death a bear-walker must go to the victim's grave to retrieve the bad medicine they used. They also take fingers and toes from the corpse and put them in bags to increase their power. Bear-walker lore is extremely similar to Apache and Navajo legends of skin-walkers in the American southwest. However, skin-walkers are almost exclusively evil.

According to one bear-walker tale, a victim's friends hid by the grave on the fourth night to wait for the bear-walker to make an appearance, hoping to discover the bear-walker's identity. As they waited, a glowing ball of fire drifted over to the grave. All became terrified and fainted except for one man. As he watched, the ball of fire turned into a bear that was breathing fire. He jumped out and grabbed hold of it. Immediately the fearsome bear vanished. The spell had been broken. In place of the bear was an old woman wearing a bearskin with buckskin bags tied to her body. He was going to kill her, but she begged and said she'd give him her powerful medicine if he spared her life. He accepted her offer, and after that he used the medicine to improve his luck and lived a charmed life.

Pakahk (also Pauguk, Paa-kuk, Pah-kack, Baykok, Baguck, Ba-kaak):

The pakahk (meaning "the emaciated one") is the "Flying Skeleton," or "Bony Specter," of Cree and Ojibwe mythology, spanning the Great Lakes region to Northern Alberta. Like the wendigo, the pakahk is associated with death, starvation, illness, and misfortune. It is often described as a flying frozen skeleton with long icy claws and eye-sockets filled with fire. There is a fair amount of overlap between concepts of the pakahk and wendigo. For example, the Ojibwe of southwestern Ontario describe the wendigo spirit as a giant skeleton of ice, much like the pakahk. Also like the wendigo, the pakahk is considered a death omen and is known for its frightful wail used to paralyze victims with fear. The sound is sometimes described as a moan or weird laughter. In 1823 explorer George Nelson stated in his journals, "They sometimes are heard during the day, and the noise is sometimes as of a quantity of dried bones rattled or shaken in a forcible manner in a kettle." Nelson notes they make a "frightful cry of heh! heh! Very quick and with abrupt termination." A pakahk's emaciated form is sometimes described as green or black with semi-translucent skin pulled tight against its bones. It is believed that when a person gets lost and dies of hunger and exposure, they may become a pakahk. The spirit flies through the night attacking its victims with a bow and arrow or a pug-ga-magan (war club). Stories regarding a pakahk's size vary from tribe to tribe. Plains Cree tales sometimes describe them as small creatures, whereas elsewhere they are human-sized.

In Nelson's journal he mentions a frightening tale told to him by a Cree man in the early 1800s. The man and a companion were camping when they woke to find a stranger sitting by their fire looking sullen with his head in his hands. "He had but skin and bone—not the least particle of flesh," Nelson recounts. "I arose; conceiving he came to ask for something to eat. I took a Beaver, cut it in two, and offered him the half of it: he did not deign to look at it—I was much afraid. I then bethought of cutting it into mouthfuls, which after presenting him I threw into the fire—thus I did with the whole; and when done, he arose and walked off peaceably in the *air*."

Traditional tales imply that pakahkwak (plural) have their own spectral tribe. The term pakahk (pauguk, baykok, etc.) is used as a general term for a class of spirit, but it is also used as a proper name for their leader, or chief—the original Pakahk manitou. Pakahk is similar to Wendigo in that they are both considered a singular powerful pawagan, manitou, or original spirit-being, but also a creature that unfortunate people may become. There is a distinction between the people who become a wendigo or a pakahk and the original powerful spirits. Thus, once-human wendigo/pakahk are related to, but not identical to, the mythical beings Pakahk and Wendigo (proper names). Unlike many indigenous spirits, Pakahk never disguises itself or transforms into the shapes of animals like many trickster spirits. It has no need for trickery and rarely speaks. It never pretends to be what it is not. It is simply fear and death, stark and inevitable.

In contrast to the wendigo, that only takes and devours, pakahk lore shows it has a beneficent side. If treated with respect and given the right offerings, (usually an animal bladder filled with bear grease), a pakahk may grant curing powers to the sick, or assist hunters in finding game and enchant their guns to always find their mark. Grease offerings are burned in a fire, as it is believed that a spirit can only accept physical material in smoke form because of its ephemeral and fleeting quality. This is how messages and offerings are passed to the realm of spirit.

Pakahk is considered the originator and patron of the Give Away Dance, or Trade Dance, conducted in its honor by the Plains Cree. During Pakahk ceremonies rifles are fired into the sky, gifts are exchanged, and children make miniature bows and arrows as offerings to Pakahk. The central feature of this ceremony is sharing of food and the exchange of gifts. According to Métis folklorist Lawrence Barkwell, "The symbolism of these feasts merges the concepts of offering, consubstantiation and creation of artificial famine, which is followed by successful hunting and trapping." In some ways, the benign side of Pakahk has Santa Claus-like characteristics, while in other tribes, Pakahk (or the many pakahkwak) is a boogeyman for children. Children are told that if they misbehave Pakahk will carry them off and eat them. This notion is very similar to Dzunukwa tales and also the Krampus figure in European Alpine Christmas traditions.

A key component to the Pakahk ceremony is a *manitohkan*, a sacred effigy, idol, or totem, representing the spirit and embodying its power. Most are carved from tree stumps and display characteristics of specific pawaganak. Usually food, tobacco, and small gifts are placed around the manitohkan as an offering. In George Nelson's journals he describes a Pakahk manitohkan used in the Pakahk ceremonial feast, "Some of them have a board about 20 or 24 ins long, flat and painted with red earth, and a head made to it of the same piece and flat as the rest. At a certain distance below the neck, as we might suppose the shoulders, are other small pieces made in the same form and about 3 or 4 ins long are stuck in each side at short distances, reaching to the ground—the lower end being small, and the head end would bear some resemblance to ribs ... a representation of the Pah-kack."

In the Autumn of 1895, while clearing the brush during the construction of St. John's Anglican mission at Wabasca, the Rev. Charles Weaver discovered a sacred Pakahk manitokan created by local Cree or Métis tribes for ceremonial rites. It was "A stump of poplar carved into the rough semblance of a head and shoulders, painted with red ochre and with three black horizontal stripes on the breast." The horizontal stripes presumably represented ribs. The

Reverend revealed his intolerance to indigenous beliefs when he penned in his journal, "Wapaskaw is a stronghold for heathen darkness." The manitokan served as a symbol to help ward off starvation. Thus, its removal and destruction were the catalyst for severe anxiety over potential famine and starvation which eventually led to full-blown wendigo panic the following year.

There are interesting parallels between Pakahk and Santa Muerte or "Holy Death," a folk saint worshiped in Central America and many parts of the United States. Like Pakahk, she is represented as a weapon-wielding skeleton (often holding an hourglass in one hand and a scythe in the other). Santa Muerte is petitioned and given offerings (usually food, money, incense, or liquor) in order to receive blessings like good luck, good health, and prosperity. Additionally, like Pakahk, she is the personification of death and can be dangerous if not treated with respect. Her darker aspect may also be invoked to hex and injure others.

American geographer, geologist, and ethnologist, Henry Schoolcraft (1793–1864) comments on Pakahk (Pauguk) in his *Myth of Hiawatha* (1856). Schoolcraft writes, "Death, where the mythos of the condition of the human frame, deprived of even the semblance of blood, and muscle, and life, is represented by the word Pauguk. Pauguk is a horrible phantom of human bones, without bones, without muscular tissue or voice, the appearance of which presages speedy dissolution. Of all the myths of the Indians, this is the most gloomy and fearful."

Roogaroo (also, Rugaru, Rougarou, Rigoureau, Rou-Garou,):
The roogaroo is a fascinating Métis and Cree hybridization of indigenous shape-shifter legends and French werewolf lore. Roogaroo is a variation of the French word *loup-garu*, meaning werewolf. The creature is not to be confused with the *rougarou* of Louisiana Cajun folklore. While both terms are very similar and have the same French origin, the cultures that use them are nearly 2,000 miles

apart and very distinct. For example, whereas the rougarou of the Cajuns is generally considered a bayou-dwelling werewolf, (often described as a bipedal humanoid with wolf-like characteristics) the roogaroo of the Métis and Cree is more of a sorcerer or shape-shifter that can turn into a wolf, a black dog, or even a black horse. Roogaroo tales are closely associated with bear-walker mythologies. Usually the only difference between the two is the form in which they choose to appear. According to legend there is one way to break the curse and turn a roogaroo back into a man; one must throw a skeleton key and hit him/her between the eyes. But be warned— one needs to keep the roogaroo's identity secret or else they will become a roogaroo.

Tupilak (also, Tupilaq):
A Tupilak is a magical creature of Inuit traditions (particularly in the Greenland area). It is a magical fetish (a talismanic carved idol or totem) that serves as a container or home for a spirit-creature. A tupilak is magically constructed by a sorcerer (called an *angakkuk* among the Inuit) with the intent to harm or destroy their enemies. The idol is typically carved out of animal parts like narwhal and walrus tusk or caribou antler—in extreme cases, even the bones of children. Tupilak carvings are generally small, usually about 3 to 8 inches tall. They are intentionally designed to represent terrifying monsters. Their fearsome expressions include prominent fangs, claws, and grim skeletal features. Most are anthropomorphic and have characteristics of arctic animals, like polar bears, seals, and walruses.

Like the golem of Jewish folklore, the figure is given life by invoking a spirit into the idol. The spirit-creature is then sent out to harm the sorcerer's target. Tupilaks are activated by placing them into the sea where it is believed they come to life and hunt down one's enemy. Like most magical attacks, it is a risky process. If the target's magical powers are stronger than the tupilak's creator, the creature could be sent back to destroy its maker.

BIBLIOGRAPHY

Chapter 1. Unthawing a Legend

Boston Daily Globe. January 19, 1886.

"Cannibalism." *Castlemaine Mount Alexander Mail.* November 25, 1859.

"Indians are." *Reno Evening Gazette.* September 12, 1912.

"Indian Windigo Superstition." *Indianapolis News.* September 1, 1899.

London American Register. January 29, 1887.

"Most Fearful." *Boston Globe.* January 11, 1920.

On-Site Research. Ross, MN. 2001. 2004. 2009. 2016.

"Ontario Indians in State of Panic." *Kalispell Daily Inter Lake.* September 14, 1912.

Smallman, Shawn. Dangerous Spirits: The Windigo in Myth and History. Heritage Press Publishing Company Ltd. 2014.

"Troop News." *Ogden Standard Examiner.* August 9, 1935.

Winnipeg Free Press. April 8, 1921.

Chapter 2. Land of the Wendigo

Barker, Clive. *Cabal.* Poseidon Press. 1988.

Berton, Pierre. *The Mysterious North.* Knopf. 1956.

Brown, Jennifer S.H. *Ojibwe Stories from the Upper Berens River: A. Irving Hallowell and Adam Bigmouth in Conversation.* University of Nebraska Press. 2018.

Cronon, William. *Uncommon Ground: Rethinking the Human Place in Nature.* W.W. Norton. *1995.*

Fessenden, Larry (editor). *A Sudden Storm—A Wendigo Reader.* Fiddleback Ltd. 2015.

Johnston, Basil. *The Manitous: The Spiritual World of the Ojibway.* Harpercollins. 1995.

Krantz, Grover. *Big Foot-Prints: A Scientific Inquiry into the Reality of Sasquatch.* Johnson Books. 1992.

Murphy, Bernice M. *The Rural Gothic in American Popular Culture: Backwoods Horrors and Terror in the Wilderness.* Palgrave Macmillan. 2013.

Norman, Howard. *Where the Chill Came From—Cree Windigo Tales and Journeys.* North Point Press. 1982.

Rayburn, Alan. *Naming Canada: Stories About Canadian Place Names.* University of Toronto Press. 2001.

W.C. Cronon. "The Trouble With Wilderness, or, Getting Back to the Wrong Nature." *Environmental History*, Vol. 1, No. 1 (Jan. 1996), 7.

Teicher, Morton I. *Windigo Psychosis: A Study of a Relationship Between Belief and Behavior Among the Indians of Northeastern Canada.* American Ethnological Society. 1960.

Thwaites, Rueben G. *The Jesuit Relations and Allied Documents.* 1896-1901.

Wonderley, Anthony. *At the Font of the Marvelous—Exploring Oral Narrative and Mythic Imagery of the Iroquois and Their Neighbors.* Syracuse University Press. 2009.

Chapter 3. Wendigo Metamorphosis: Going Wendigo

Alexander, Henry. *Travels and Adventures in Canada and the Indian Territories between the Years 1760 and 1776.* 1809.

Brightman, Robert A. "The Wendigo in the Material World." *Ethnohistory.* 1988.

Bishop, Charles A. (ed. Thomas R. Williams) "Northern Algonkian Cannibalism and Windigo Psychosis." *Psychological Anthropology*: 237-248. 1975.

Brown, Jennifer S.H. *Ojibwe Stories from the Upper Berens River: A. Irving Hallowell and Adam Bigmouth in Conversation.* University of Nebraska Press. 2018.

Brown, Jennifer (with Robert Brightman), *The Orders of the Dreamed: George Nelson on Cree and Northern Ojibwe Religion and Myth*, 1823. University of Manitoba Press. 1988.

Jennes, Diamond. "The Ojibwa Indians of Perry Sound, Their Social and Religious Life." National Museum of Canada , Bulletin No. 78, Anthropological Series No. 17. 1935.

Kohl, Johann Georg. *Kitchi-Gami - Life Among the Lake Superior Ojibway.* Minnesota Historical Press. 1985.

Landes, Ruth. *Ojibwa Religion and the Midewiwin.* University of Wisconsin Press. 1968.

Lowery, Bob. "Traditional Native Way of Life in Northern Manitoba—Fond Memories for one of Canada's Oldest." *Winnipeg Free Press.* November 30, 1979.

Ibid. "Okimow of North Claims 'Devil Persons' on Decline." *Winnipeg Free Press.* February 13, 1982.

Norman, Howard. *Where the Chill Came From—Cree Windigo Tales and Journeys.* North Point Press. 1982.

Preston, Richard. "The Witiko: Algonkian Knowledge and White-man Knowledge," in *Manlike Monsters on Trial: Early Records and Modern Evidence*, ed. Marjorie M. Halpin and Michael M. Ames. Univ of British Columbia Press. 1980.

Ray, Carl. (with James R. Stevens). *Sacred Legends.* Penumbra Press. 1995.

Rohrl, Vivian J. "A Nutritional Factor in Windigo Psychosis" in *American Anthropologist New Serie*s, Vol. 72, No. 1 (Feb., 1970), pp. 97-101.

Smallman, Shawn. *Dangerous Sprits: The Windigo in Myth and History.* Heritage House Publishing Company. 2015

Smith, James G.E. "Notes on Witiko." In *Papers of the Seventh Algonquian Conference*, edited by William Cowan. Carleton University. 1976.

Chapter 4. Territory of Terror: Alberta, Canada

"A Prisoners Escape." *Rapid City Spectator.* October 27, 1887.

"A Trout Lake Tragedy." *Glenboro Gazette.* May 8, 1896.

"A 'Wehtiko' Must Be Killed." *Winnipeg Tribune.* August 22, 1899.

"A Wendigo Murdered by His Companions for Their Own Safety." *Glenboro Gazette.* May 8, 1896.

"Arrest at Slave Lake." *Fort MacLeod Gazette.* October 18, 1887.

"Cannibalism in Canada." *Charlestown Hoosier Democrat.* May 26, 1899.

Carlson, Nathan. "Reviving the Wihtikow: Cannibal Monsters in Northern Alberta Cree and Métis Cosmology." Undergraduate Thesis, University of Alberta. 2005.

Carlson, Nathan. "Reviving Witiko (Windigo): An Ethnohistory of 'Cannibal Monsters' in the Athabasca District of Northern Alberta, 1878-1910." *Ethnohistory.* 2009.

"Devil Worship Among the Cree." *Calgary Herald.* August 24, 1907.

Edmonton Bulletin. July 17, 1899.

"Exorcism Tried in Vain, Axe Supplemented Medicine." *Vancouver Daily World.* September 13, 1899.

"For Killing a Witch." *Winona Daily Republican.* October 22, 1887.

"From Lesser Slave Lake." *Edmonton Bulletin.* May 8, 1899.

"Horrible Sacrifices." *Ogden Herald.* November 8, 1887.

"Indian Murder Trial." *Edmonton Bulletin.* August 14, 1899.

"Killed by Her Husband and Son by Her Request." *Columbus Enquirer Sun.* November 5, 1887.

"Killed His Wife." *Winnipeg Free Press.* October 1, 1887.

"Indian Windigo Superstition." *Indianapolis News.* September 1, 1899.

Lorentzen, Pearl. Personal Interview. 2019.

"Manslaughter." *Winnipeg Tribune*. August 15, 1899.

"More Indian Murders." *Edmonton Bulletin*. June 12, 1899.

"Northwest Territories." *Victoria Daily Colonist*. October 27, 1887.

On-Site Research / Interviews. 2019.

QuAppelle Vidette. November 24, 1887.

Saint Joseph Weekly Gazette. March 22, 1888.

"Starving Indians." *Plattsburg Republican*. February 5, 1887.

"The Legend of Eating Creek." *Lakeside Leader*. January 8, 1992.

"Wapisca." *Edmonton Bulletin*. April 16, 1896.

"Witch Killing in Canada." *New Haven Daily Morning Journal and Courier*. October 16, 1899.

Chapter 5. Cannibalistic Chaos: The Gruesome Tale of Swift Runner

"A Hungry Cannibal." *Richmond Daily Dispatch*. December 31, 1879.

"A Very Remarkable Execution." *Weekly Reno Gazette*. February 12, 1880.

"An Indian's Horrible Crime." *Jackson Sentinel*. January 29, 1880.

"Canadian Mail." *Victoria Daily British Colonist*. January 14, 1880.

"Cannibalism." *Kingston Daily British Whig.* July 30.1879.

"Cannibalism." *Savannah Morning News.* February 27,1880.

Carlson, Nathan. "Reviving the Wihtikow: Cannibal Monsters in Northern Alberta Cree and Métis Cosmology." Undergraduate Thesis, University of Alberta. 2005.

"Criminal Court Business." *Winnipeg Free Press.* September 25, 1879.

Carlson, Nathan. "Reviving Witiko (Windigo): An Ethnohistory of Cannibal Monsters in the Athabasca District of Northern Alberta, 1878-1910." *Ethnohistory.* 2009.

"Exit the Swift Runner." *Battleford Saskatchewan Herald.* January 12, 1880.

"Hanging a Cannibal." *Hoboken Advertiser.* January 17, 1880.

"Hanging an Indian." *Hermann Advertiser Courier.* January 21, 1880.

"Horrible Cannibalism." *Branford Gleaner.* August 13, 1879.

"Horrible Crime." *Absecon South Jersey Republican.* January 31, 1880.

"How They Gathered Him." *Winnipeg Free Press.* January 16, 1880.

"Indian Cannibal Executed." *Galveston Daily News.* January 1, 1880.

Indian Journal. February 12, 1880.

"Indians Total Abstainers." *New Castle News.* October 29, 1935.

"Sad Case of Cannibalism." *Battleford Saskatchewan Herald.* June 30, 1879.

"Swift Runner." *Brooklyn Daily Eagle*. January 15, 1880.

"The First Legal Execution." *Vancouver Independent.*

"The Indian Cannibal." *Macon Georgia Weekly Telegraph and Georgia Journal and Messenger.* January 6, 1880.

"The Indian Who Ate His Family." *Logan Hocking Sentinel.* February 5, 1880.

"The Recent Hanging of Swift Runner." *Savannah Morning News*. January 28, 1880.

Thomson, Colin. *Swift Runner*. Detselig Enterprises Limited. 1984.

Chapter 6. The Last Wendigo Hunter: The Life and Death of Jack Fiddler

"Accused Red Man Suicided." *Brandon Weekly Sun*. October 10, 1907.

"Commute the Sentence." *Winnipeg Tribune*. December 12, 1907.

"Cree Chiefs on Trial for Murder." *Winnipeg Free Press*. August 7, 1907.

Fiddler, Thomas & Steven, James. *Killing the Shamen*. Penumbra Press. 1985

"Fiendish Work of Northern Indians." *Brandon Weekly Sun*. October 17, 1907.

"Indian Must Die." *The Gazette*. October 16, 1907.

"Joseph Pa-Cje-Quan is Sentenced to Death." *Winnipeg Tribune*. October 15, 1907.

"Murder Done by Indian Custom." *Fort Wayne Journal Gazette.* August 21, 1907.

"Murders Daughter to Cast Out Evil." *Shelbyville Democrat.* November 21, 1907.

"Possessed of the Devil." *The Gazette.* October 8, 1907.

"Practice Revolting Cruelty." *Racine Daily Journal.* October 17, 1907.

"Punishment for Stranglers." *Waterloo Daily Courier.* October 16, 1907.

"Remarkable Admission." *Winnipeg Free Press.* October 16, 1907.

Smallman, Shawn. *Dangerous Spirits: The Windigo in Myth and History.* Heritage Press Publishing Company Ltd. 2014.

"Strangler Chief Dies at New Year." *Winnipeg Free Press.* October 16, 1907.

"To Stop Devil Worship." *Washington Post.* October 20, 1907.

"Try Indian Medicine Man." *The Billings Gazette.* August 20, 1907.

"Wholesale Murder." *The Gazette.* October 8, 1907.

Chapter 7. Hatchets, Tallow, and Ice: Surviving Lake Windigo

Marsh, Otis. *The Haunts of Star Island.* 1989.

Minnesota Historical Society. *Star Island Oral History Project.* 1976, 1985.

On-Site Research/Interviews. 2013, 2015, 2016, 2019.

Pammel, L.H. *The Flora of Star Island and Vicinity.* Iowa State University. 1915.

Ryan, Carol. *Star Island: A Minnesota Summer Community.* Pogo Press. 2001.

"Ripley's Believe It or Not!" *Anderson Sunday Herald.* July 20, 1958.

"The Wendigo." *In Search of Monsters.* 2019.

Chapter8. The Omen of Death is Coming: The Wendigo of Ross, Minnesota

Chapin, Earl. *The Early History of the Roseau Valley.* Minnesota History. 1943.

Lewis, Chad. *The Minnesota Road Guide to Mysterious Creatures.* On The Road Publications. 2001.

Lewis, Chad & Fisk, Terry. *The Minnesota Road Guide to Haunted Locations.* Unexplained Publishing. 2005.

Nelson, Jake. *Forty Years in the Roseau Valley. Roseau County Historical Society.*

On-Site Research by Author. 2004, 2006, 2009, 2011, 2013, 2015, 2018.

Chapter 9. A Battle of Sanity and Soul: Windigo Psychosis and the Broader Psychology Surrounding Belief in the Wendigo

Brown, Jennifer & Brightman, Robert. *"The Orders of the Dreamed": George Nelson on Cree and Northern Ojibwa Religion and Myth, 1823.* Minnesota Historical Society Press. 1988.

American Psychiatric Association. *Diagnostic and Statistical Manual of Mental Disorders. 5ᵗʰ Edition.* 2019.

American Psychological Association. *APA Dictionary of Psychology.* 2019. https://dictionary.apa.org

Boston Daily Globe. January 19, 1886.

"Cannibal Indian at Large." *New York Times.* March 13, 1904.

Citro, Joseph A. *The Vermont Monster Guide.* University Press of New England. 2009.

"Crees Displeased Tribal God." *Brandon Daily Sun.* October 28, 1932.

"Demon Awes Indians." *Edmonton Journal.* October 28, 1931.

"Didn't Eat His Family." *The Wahpeton Times.* March 18, 1904.

"Find Mental Disease Among Primitive Men." *El Paso Herald Post.* January 9, 1934.

"Grotesque Monster Haunted the Tamarak Forests of Canada." *Hartford Courant.* August 10, 1931.

"Indian is a Cannibal." *Brainerd Daily Dispatch.* March 12, 1904.

"Indian Murder Trial." *Edmonton Bulletin.* August 14, 1899.

"Indian Windigo Superstition." *Indianapolis News.* September 1, 1899.

"Killed by Her Husband and Son by Her Request." *Columbus Enquirer Sun.* November 5, 1887.

Lewis, Chad. "Investigating Students' Belief in the Paranormal." Master's Thesis, University of Wisconsin-Stout. 2004.

London American Register. January 29, 1887.

"Ontario Indians in State of Panic." *Kalispell Daily Inter Lake.* September 14, 1912.

Marano, Lou. "Windigo Psychosis: The Anatomy of an Emic—Etic Confusion." *Current Anthropology, 23*(4). 1982.

"Murders Daughter to Cast Out Devil." *Shelbyville Democrat.* November 21, 1907.

"Punishment for Stranglers." *Waterloo Daily Courier.* October 16, 1907.

"Shot Their Chief." *Logansport Times.* November 3, 1899.

"Takes Lots of Whiskey to Beat Wendigo." *Winnipeg Tribune.* January 31, 1947.

Teicher, Morton. *Windigo Psychosis: A Study of a Relationship Between Belief and Behavior Among the Indians of Northeastern Canada.* American Ethnological Society. 1960.

"The Indian Who Ate His Family." *Logan Hocking Sentinel.* February 5, 1880.

"To Stop Devil Worship." *Washington Post.* October 20, 1907.

"Twisted Her Hair." *Newark Daily Advocate.* December 15, 1897.

Rohrl, Vivian. "A Nutritional Factor in Windigo Psychosis." *American Anthropologist* New Series, Vol. 72, No. 1. 1970.

"She-Ma-Gan." *Biloxi Herald.* March 20, 1895.

Simmons, Ronald & Hughes, Charles. *The Culture-Bound Syndromes: Folk Illinesses of Psychiatric and Anthropological Interest.* D. Reidel Publishing Company. 1985.

"Starving Indians." *Plattsburg Republican.* February 5, 1887.

Waldram, James. *Revenge of the Windigo: The Construction of the Mind and Mental Health of North American Aboriginal Peoples.* University of Toronto Press. 2004.

"Wapisca." *Edmonton Bulletin.* April 16, 1896.

"Wholesale Murder." *The Gazette.* October 8, 1907.

Winnipeg Free Press. April 8, 1921.

"'Witiko' Fears Stalk Indians of Northwoods." *The News Journal.* March 10, 1933.

Wonderley, Anthony. *At the Font of the Marvelous.* Syracuse University Press. 2009.

Chapter 10. Curing the Wendigo Curse

Barnouw, Victor. *Wisconsin Chippewa Myths and Tales: And Their Relation to Chippewa Life.* University of Wisconsin Press. 1977.

Brizinski, Morris and Savage, Howard. "Dog Sacrifices among the Algonkian Indians: An Example from the Frank Bay Site." *Ontario Archaeology.* 1983.

Brown, Jennifer & Brightman, Robert. *"The Orders of the Dreamed": George Nelson on Cree and Northern Ojibwa Religion and Myth, 1823.* Minnesota Historical Society Press. 1988.

Bushnell, David Ives. "Native Cemeteries and Forms of Burial East of the Mississippi." *Bureau of American Ethnology Bulletin.* 1920.

"Cannibalism." *Castlemaine Mount Alexander Mail.* November 25, 1859.

"Cannibalism in Canada." *Charlestown Hoosier Democrat.* May 26, 1899.

"Defence Of An Indian Custom." *Winnipeg Free Press.* August 31, 1907.

"Demon Awes Indians." *Edmonton Journal.* October 28, 1931.

Edmonton Bulletin. March 15, 1897.

Fiddler, Thomas & Steven, James. *Killing the Shamen.* Penumbra Press. 1985.

"From the Diary of a Hudson's Bay Clerk in the Seventies." *Creston Review.* December 03, 1920.

"Grotesque Monster Haunted the Tamarak Forests of Canada." *Hartford Courant.* August 10, 1931.

"Horrible Sacrifices." *Ogden Herald.* November 8, 1887.

"Indian Windigo Superstition." *Indianapolis News.* September 1, 1899.

"Killed by Her Husband and Son by Her Request." *Columbus Enquirer Sun.* November 5, 1887.

Landes, Ruth. *The Ojibwa Woman.* Columbia University Press. 1938.

"Murder Done by Indian Custom." *Fort Wayne Journal Gazette.* Aug 21, 1907.

Norman, Howard. *Where the Chill Came From: Cree Windigo Tales and Journeys.* North Point Press. 1982.

"Practice Revolting Cruelty." *Racine Daily Journal.* October 17, 1907.

"She-Ma-Gan." *Biloxi Herald.* March 20, 1895.

"Takes Lots of Whiskey to Beat Wendigo." *Winnipeg Tribune.* January 31, 1947.

"The Cheerful Philosopher." *Winnipeg Free Press.* April 8, 1921.

"Wapisca." *Edmonton Bulletin.* April 16, 1896.

Winnipeg Free Press. April 8, 1921.

"'Witiko' Fears Stalk Indians of Northwoods." *The News Journal.* March 10, 1933.

Chapter 11. Melting Hearts of Ice: How to Kill a Wendigo

"A Very Remarkable Execution." *Weekly Reno Gazette.* February 12, 1880.

"A 'Wehtiko' Must Be Killed." *Winnipeg Tribune.* August 22, 1899.

Boston Daily Globe. January 19, 1886.

Brown, Jennifer. *Ojibwe Stories from the Upper Berens River: A. Irving Hallowell and Adam Bigmouth in Conversation.* University of Nebraska. 2018.

"Cannibalism." *Castlemaine Mount Alexander Mail.* November 25, 1859.

"Cannibalism in Canada." *Charlestown Hoosier Democrat.* May 26, 1899.

"Demon Awes Indians." *Edmonton Journal.* October 28, 1931.

"Devil Worship Among the Cree." *Calgary Herald.* August 24, 1907.

"Exorcism Tried in Vain, Axe Supplemented Medicine." *Vancouver Daily World.* September 13, 1899.

"Fiendish Work of Northern Indians." *Brandon Weekly Sun*. October 17, 1907.

"From the Diary of a Hudson's Bay Clerk in the Seventies." *Creston Review*. December 03, 1920.

"Grotesque Monster Haunted the Tamarak Forests of Canada." *Hartford Courant*. August 10, 1931.

"Horrible Murder." *Glenboro Gazette*. December 24, 1897.

"Horrible Sacrifices." *Ogden Herald*. November 8, 1887.

Indian Journal. February 12, 1880.

"Indian Murder Trial." *Edmonton Bulletin*. August 14, 1899.

"Indian Must Die." *The Gazette*. October 16, 1907.

"Indian Windigo Superstition." *Indianapolis News*. September 1, 1899.

"Joseph Pa-Cje-Quan is Sentenced to Death." *Winnipeg Tribune*. October 15, 1907.

"Killed by Her Husband and Son by Her Request." *Columbus Enquirer Sun*. November 5, 1887.

"Killed the 'Evil Spirit.'" *Winnipeg Free Press*. October 28, 1899.

"Killed a Wendigo." *Hamiota Herald*. November 7, 1899.

Landes, Ruth. *The Ojibwa Woman*. Columbia University Press. 1938.

"Manslaughter." *Winnipeg Tribune*. August 15, 1899.

"Murder Done by Indian Custom." *Fort Wayne Journal Gazette*. Aug 21, 1907.

Norman, Howard. *Where the Chill Came From: Cree Windigo Tales and Journeys*. North Point Press. 1982.

"Practice Revolting Cruelty." *Racine Daily Journal*. October 17, 1907.

"Punishment for Stranglers." *Waterloo Daily Courier*. October 16, 1907.

Ramsland, Katherine. *The Science of Vampires*. Berkley. 2002.

"She-Ma-Gan." *Biloxi Herald*. March 20, 1895.

"Shot Their Chief." *Logansport Times*. November 3, 1899.

Smallman, Shawn. *Dangerous Spirits: The Windigo in Myth and History*. Heritage Press Publishing Company Ltd. 2014.

"Takes Lots of Whiskey to Beat Wendigo." *Winnipeg Tribune*. January 31, 1947.

"The Great Northland: The West's Last Frontier." *Edmonton Bulletin*. February 10, 1923.

"The Indian Who Ate His Family." *Logan Hocking Sentinel*. February 5, 1880.

Thomson, Colin. *Swift Runner*. Detselig Enterprises Limited. 1984.

"To Stop Devil Worship." *Washington Post*. October 20, 1907.

"Try Indian Medicine Man." *The Billings Gazette*. August 20, 1907.

"Twisted Her Hair." *Newark Daily Advocate*. December 15, 1897.

Tyrrell, Joseph Burr. *David Thompson's Narrative Of His Explorations In Western America, 1784-1812 (1916)*. Kessinger Publishing. 2010.

"Shot Their Chief." *Logansport Times*. November 3, 1899.

QuAppelle Vidette. November 24, 1887.

"Wapisca." *Edmonton Bulletin.* April 16, 1896.

"Wholesale Murder." *The Gazette.* October 8, 1907.

Winnipeg Free Press. April 8, 1921.

"'Witiko' Fears Stalk Indians of Northwoods." *The News Journal.* March 10, 1933.

Chapter 12. The Modern Man-Eater: The Wendigo Legend Today

Atwood, Margaret. *Strange Things—The Malevolent North in Canadian Literature.* Clarendon Press. 1995.

Blackwood, Algernon. "The Wendigo." *The Lost Valley and Other Stories.* Eveleigh Nash. 1910.

Brightman, Robert A. "The Wendigo in the Material World." *Ethnohistory.* 1988.

Burgesse, J.A. "The Windigo." *The Beaver.* March 26, 1947, 4.

Cameron, Duncan. "A Sketch of the Customs, Manners, and Way of Living of the Natives in the Barren Country about Nipigon." *Les Bourgeois de la Campagnie du Nord-Quest,* L.R. Masson (editor). De L'imprimerie General A. Cote at C. 1890.

CBS News. "Greyhound killer believed man he beheaded was an alien." https://www.cbc.ca/news/canada/manitoba/greyhound-killer-believed-man-he-beheaded-was-an-alien-1.1131575. Accessed 12/14/2019.

Colombo, John Robert. *Windigo: An Anthology of Fact and Fiction.* Prairie Books. 1982.

Egerkrans, Johan. *The Undead.* B. Wahlstroms Bokforlag. 2018.

Falconer, William. Hudson's Bay Archives, B198/a/19.

Fessenden, Larry (editor). *A Sudden Storm—A Wendigo Reader.* Fiddleback Ltd. 2015.

Forbes, Jack D. *Columbus and Other Cannibals: The Wetiko Disease of Exploitation, Imperialism, and Terrorism.* Seven Stories Press. 2008.

Guinard, Joseph E. "Witiko among the Tete-de-Boule," *Primitive Man,* Vol. 3, No. 3/4 (Jul. - Oct., 1930), pp. 69-71.

Johnston, Basil. *The Manitous: The Spiritual World of the Ojibway.* Harpercollins. 1995.

King, Stephen. *The Shining.* Random House, 1977.

Krueger, William Kent. *Iron Lake.* Atria. 1998.

Leland, Charles G. *Algonquin Legends of New England.* 1884.

Levy, Paul. *Dispelling Wetiko—Breaking the Curse of Evil.* North Atlantic Books. 2013.

Norman, Howard. *Where the Chill Came From—Cree Windigo Tales and Journeys.* North Point Press. 1982.

Pinkerton, Katherine. *Windigo.* Harcourt, Brace and Comany. 1945.

Plant, John. "The Plains Indian Clowns, Their Contraries and Related Phenomena," 2010. URL: http://www.anjol.de/documents/100703_heyoka_article_johnplant.pdf

Richardson, Charles. *A New Dictionary of the English Language.* 1839.

Smallman, Shawn. *Dangerous Sprits: The Windigo in Myth and History.* Heritage House Publishing Company. 2015.

Twaites, Reuben Gold (editor). *The Jesuit Relations and Allied Documents*, vol. 46. Burrows Brothers. 1899.

Chapter 13. Cannibal Counterparts: Similar Creatures of the Northwoods

Brown, Jennifer S.H. *Ojibwe Stories from the Upper Berens River: A. Irving Hallowell and Adam Bigmouth in Conversation.* University of Nebraska Press. 2018.

Cooper, John M. "The Cree Witiko Psychosis." *Primitive Man* 6, no. 1. 1933.

Dorson, Richard M. *Bloodstoppers and Bearwalkers: Folk Traditions of the Upper Peninsula.* Harvard University Press. 1952.

Godfrey, Linda. *American Monsters.* TarcherPerigee. 2014.

Johnson, Basil H. *The Bear-Walker and Other Stories.* Royal Ontario Musuem. 1995.

Kohl, Johann Georg. *Kitchi-Gami - Life Among the Lake Superior Ojibway. Minnesota Historical Press.* 1985.

Leland, Charles G. *Algonquin Legends of New England.* 1884.

Norman, Howard. *Where the Chill Came From—Cree Windigo Tales and Journeys.* North Point Press. 1982.

Ridington, Robin. "A Comparison of Cannibal Belief among Boreal Forest Athapaskans and Algonkians." *Anthropologica*, New Series, Vol. 18, No. 2 (1976), pp. 107-129.

Sanday, Peggy Reeves. *Divine Hunger: Cannibalism as a Cultural System.* Cambridge University Press. 1986.

Schoolcraft, Henry R. *The Myth of Hiawatha, and Other Oral Legends, Mythologic and Allegoric, of the North American Indians*. J.B. Lippincott & Co. 1856.

Speck, Frank G. "Penobscot Tales and Religious Beliefs." The Journal of American Folklore.Vol. 48, No. 187 (Jan. – Mar., 1935).

Wonderley, Anthony. *At the Font of the Marvelous: Exploring Oral Narrative and Mythic Imagery of the Iroquois and Their Neighbors*. Syracuse University Press. 2009.

MORE INFORMATION ABOUT THE ARTWORK

Adrian Day linktr.ee/adrians_anomalies

Alexey Monzhaley deviantart.com/monopteryx

Eric Franer deviantart.com/franeres

IrenHorrors deviantart.com/irenhorrors

JamieSnellArt etsy.com/shop/JamieSnellArt

Johnny Sixgun

Lee Howard etsy.com/shop/QuietRoomBears

Phyllis Galde and Fate Magazine www.fatemag.com

RF Pangborn www.instagram.com/pangbornrf

Rick Fisk www.rickfiskphotos.com

Sarah Terrell www.sarahterrellillustration.com

ABOUT THE AUTHORS

CHAD LEWIS

Born and raised in the legend-filled Northwoods of Wisconsin, Chad's background is in the field of Psychology. Chad focused his undergraduate and graduate work on applying psychological concepts to his research into the supernatural, focusing his master's thesis on assessing students' belief in the paranormal.

Chad has spent the last 25 years traveling the world researching human perception, human belief systems, superstitions, and folklore. Chad has authored over 20 books on the supernatural and extensively lectures on these topics. The more bizarre the legend is, the more likely you will find Chad there.

KEVIN LEE NELSON

Kevin Lee Nelson grew up in Wisconsin surrounded by lumberjack lore and tales of Northwoods monsters. The rich folklore of the Great Lakes region made a deep impression on him which continues to the present. He continually travels the nation seeking out and recording America's hidden legends and vanishing folklore. As a student of American folk-magic traditions and Western esotericism, Kevin's unconventional perspectives allow him to uncover and decipher symbolic information often hidden within events of high strangeness.

Kevin has investigated hauntings on ABC's *Scariest Places on Earth*, searched for werewolves on Discovery Channel's *Mystery Hunters*, and tracked vampirism on Discovery Channel's *Travelers*. He has professionally lectured at paranormal conferences for over two decades. He is the co-author of *The Van Meter Visitor: A True and Mysterious Encounter with the Unknown* and *The Big Muddy Monster: Legends, Sightings, and Other Strange Encounters*. Kevin is a founding member of Back Roads Lore, a research collective dedicated to chronicling anomalous events, historical mysteries, urban legends, and the darker side of folklore. His personal mission is to seek out, record, and preserve our rich heritage of legends and lore.